Nexus of Productive Modern Energy Uses

Assessing the Planning, Financing, Policy and Behavioral Imperatives

I0420989

Amos Yesutanbul Nkpeebo

Research Group on Clean Development

ReGCDEV, Ghana

Published By

Research Group on Clean Development

ReGCDEV, Ghana

Research Group on Clean Development (ReGCDEV) is a subsidiary of Clean Development International (CDI). ReGCDEV has the privilege of working with thousands of experts from all over the world, passionate about environmental improvement and its importance for human well-being.

Abstract

The energy challenges within developing countries are vast and varied yet in examining the financing nexus, there is a pervasive line of similarities. Largely, energy policy focus has been skewed towards institutional and human resource capacity building as well as regulatory reforms required to create an enabling environment. There are quite some variations. Nonetheless the eminent obstacle to achieving policy goals has been the issue of cost recovery. The recent increase of oil and gas reserves constitute a structural variable in energy policy and governance. Growing attention to issues of governance as they relate to energy at the regional, national as well as local levels need to be addressed taking into consideration the fact that there are no "easy fix" solutions to the challenges. In order to address this and related challenges, integrated resource and resiliency planning is prerequisite in the generation, transmission, and distribution sectors; transitioning to wholesale electricity markets; distribution and commercial loss reduction; promotion of energy efficiency and demand-side management; and support for the expansion of renewable energy projects. The underlying question remains that what are the required, financing, planning and policy apparatuses? It is vital to recommend that energy producers and distributors like Kenya Power or Electricity Company of Ghana (ECG) need to re-evaluate the energy-user threshold in order to develop a viable energy mix that meets the needs of the urban consumer as well as rural catchments like Ngaciuma-Kinyaritha in Kenya. At the household level and in the rural household economy, there are a plethora of variables that are still less understood. This accounts for the inadequate business proof for green mini-grids (GMGs) in Ghana, for instance. Energy-finance modelling LEAP/ETM systems would facilitate the effective deployment of village or district level electrical distribution systems like mini-grids. Mini-grids are becoming increasingly recognised as an essential part of a comprehensive strategy to achieve universal energy access. This is not exactly diametric to the current financing approaches that tend focus on conventional fossil fuel dependent energy sources. As evidenced in its policy context, a part of the energy challenge in Ghana is the overemphasis on accessibility. Like other developing countries, Ghana's current energy challenge is very much of access as it is of reliability, scalability and productivity gains resulting from increasing energy access. These and other imperatives relating to integrative resource planning, financing and environmental behavior constitute the key underpins of the burgeoning debate on the significance of rural energy financing and by extension GMGs deployment in Sub Saharan Africa. A profitable and sustainable deployment of GMGs is highly contingent on capacity for productive energy uses with emphasis on the finance, planning, behavioural and policy imperatives- an expanse that still requires significant research, demonstration and development.

ACKNOWLEDGEMENTS

Prima facea, I am grateful to God for the good health and wellbeing that were necessary to complete this book.

I place on record, my sincere thank you to Professor Chris Shisanya and Professor Joy Obando, Dr. I.O Mahiri, and Dr. Cush Luwesi Ngonzo of the Geography Department, Kenyatta University for their continuous encouragement. I wish to express my sincere thanks to Prof. Dr. mult. Dr. h.c. Müfit Bahadir, Technische Universität Braunschweig, Germany; Dr. Theo Anderson, FoE-Ghana; Mr. P. A. Anokye, Planning Department, KNUST; Dr. Matyn Davies, Frontier Advisory, S.A; and Dr. Eric Thomas, ETA, USA for providing me with all the necessary advice and facilities for the research. I am extremely thankful and indebted to you for sharing expertise and valuable guidance and encouragement with me.

I am also grateful to my very colleagues, Juveanry Madyanga, Catherine Mwingira, and Samuel Norvixoxo, Francis Addy, Clement Mensah and all others. I take this opportunity to express gratitude to all of the Research Group on Clean Development (ReGCDEV) members, Mutatio Institute Research Team for their help and support. I also thank my parents for the unceasing encouragement, support and attention. I am also grateful to my partner who supported me through this venture.

I also place on record, my sense of gratitude to one and all, who directly or indirectly, have learnt their hand in this venture.

Acronyms and Abbreviations

AEI	Alternative Energy Institute
ATP	Ability To Pay
B/C	Benefit per Cost
BCR	Benefit Cost Ratio
CDM	Clean Development Mechanisms
DNA	Designated National Authority
ECG	Electricity Company of Ghana
ETM	Energy Transition Model
FGD(s)	Focused Group Discussion(s)
GEF	Global Energy Facility
GEDAP	Ghana Energy Development and Access Project
GHG	Green House Gas
GRIDCO	Grid Development Company
GSGDA	Ghana Shared Growth and Development Agenda
GVEP	Global Village Energy Partnership
H.E.P	Hydro Electric Power
IAP	Integrated Assessment and Planning
IWRM	Integrated Water Resource Management
LPG	Liquefied Petroleum Gas
Ksh	Kenya Shillings
KPLC	Kenya Power and Lighting Company
MOE	Ministry of Energy
MKEPP	Mount Kenya East Pilot Project
MDG	Millennium Development Goals
NCSA	National Capacity Needs Self-Assessment
NEMA	National Environmental Management Authority
NGOs	Non-Governmental Organization
NPV	Net Present Value
PV	Photovoltaic

PCE	Perceived Consumer Effect
PESTELI	Political, Economic, Social, Technological, Environmental, Legal and Institutional
TAPCO	Takoradi Power Company
TICO	Takoradi International Company
TTPP	Tema Thermal Power Plant
PUE	Productive Uses of Energy
PURC	Public Utility Regulation Commission
RETs	Renewable Energy Technologies
SACCO	Savings and Credit Co-operative
SE4ALL	Sustainable Energy for All
SEAAF	Sustainable Energy for All Acceleration Framework
SECO	Swiss Agency for Economic Affairs
SHEP	Self-Help Electrification Project
SMEs	Small and Medium Enterprises
SHS	Solar Home Systems
SPSS	Statistical Package for Social Sciences
UNEP	United Nations Environmental Program
VC	Venture Capitalist
WEDI	Women Enterprise Development Institute
WRUA	Water Resource User Association

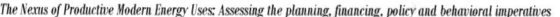

The Planning Imperative

Planning the Deployment of PV Solar Energy in the Rural Economy Using the case of Ngaciuma-Kinyarither Sub-Catchment in Kenya

By

Amos Yesutanbul Nkpeebo

Research Group on Clean Development

ReGCDEV, Ghana

At a glance

Harnessing rural development potential with turnkey modern energy

Globally, Renewable electricity sector grew by 26% between 2005 and 2010 globally and currently provides about 20% of the world's total power (including hydro-power). Rural areas attract a large part of investment related to renewable energy deployment, tending to be sparsely populated but with abundant sources of renewable electricity. The Kenyan energy mix is quite vast. Yet the rural population which constitutes the majority (over 70%) is highly deprived of energy for development loosely premised on a presumed unavailability of effective energy demand in rural areas. The greenness of this argument is quite apparent in its short-termism agenda. The disposable income of rural households is developing fast due to increasing access to economic opportunities in Africa and Kenya. As a result, small households are able to acquire and install solar panels for their domestic lighting. This study posits the availability of a reasonably mature energy market potential for rural households in Kenya. However, the current pattern of commercial energy-oriented development, particularly focused on fossil fuels and centralized electricity generation, has resulted in large proportions of rural populations and urban poor continue to depend on low quality energy sources and high fuel-consuming devices, leading to low a quality of life. The current status is largely a result of adoption of centralized energy planning, which ignores energy use potentials of the rural areas and poor. Using PESTELI analysis, the study perceived a tenable potential in rural energy supply and recommends the strengthening of decentralized energy planning, energy user remodelling and integrated resource planning and capacity building approaches among others. It also recommended that the Ministry of energy (MoE) in collaboration with Global Village Energy Partnership (GVEP) could pilot alternate capacity building scenarios based on integrated sub-catchment management approach. It highlights in conclusion that the intractability of rural household energy markets in Sub Saharan Africa, still lie in the paucity and inadequacy of empirical data on the rural household energy economy.

Content

1.0 Introduction to Local Energy Economy and Alternatives

1.1 Background

Over the years, solar energy has become a central to the climate change adaptation debate. It is however interesting to note that Photovoltaic (PV) Solar Home Systems (SHS), which since the 1980s, has proven a potential solution to the overreliance on woodfuels and paraffin is still challenged by profound systemic inefficiencies. Jacobson (2006) and Owusu (2010) exemplified that, owing to varying household financial capabilities, solar energy is seen to have relatively poor demand, less economic value and little environmental significance. In the context of existing financing models, solar energy application is apparently restricted to household lighting and a few heating processes. Cory and Coughlin (2009) attempts to address this phenomenon by providing some "new financial models" including monetizing environmental values. In the context of residential deployment of PV solar, the generalized approaches tend to gloss over critical variables within the household energy economy which result in result PV solar home systems deployment or solar electricity contributing insignificant productivity gains in the local development framework. In Kenya for instance, the demand for solar PV systems is found to be driven by middle class purchasing power made up of small business owners, rural professionals such as school teachers, civil servants, and pastors, as well as the better off among the small holder cash cropping farmers (Jacobson 2004). In supporting these observations, this paper highlights some essential gaps in in PV solar deployment in order to attenuate this challenge in terms of effectiveness, efficiency, equity, institutional feasibility and replicability.

2.0 Research Design and Methods Adopted

A multi-stage sampling methodology was used as the population was deemed to have a more elaborate sample frame (Kumekpor, 2002). One hundred (100) households were randomly selected and distributed proportionately among 9 randomly selected communities in the upper, middle and lower zones of the Ngaciuma Kinyarither Sub-catchment. This technique ensured that every sample element had equal opportunities of being selected. In each of the three zones, 10 households were purposively selected for an FGD to provide insight for analysing scenarios generated.

3.0 Results and Discussions

3.1 How Much It Cost to Shift to Alternative Energy Sources

The study observed the compared solar Pv cost in Kenya with that general solar Pv costs in Africa and that of the world. It indicated that in the context of Africa, Kenya is experiencing the widest penetration levels of solar Pv systems and that the high rate of solar Pv installations is accompanied or driven by relatively lower prices. This was also illustrated by Ondraczek (2013) as seen in figure 3.1.

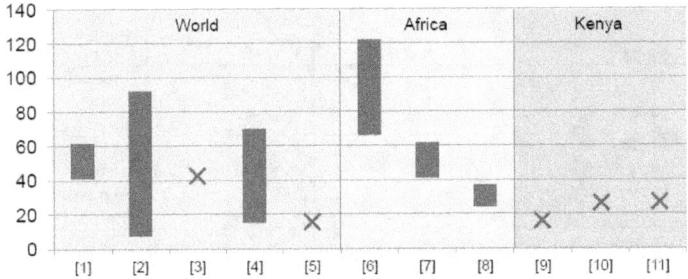

Figure 3.1: Solar electricity generation cost estimates

Source: Janosch Ondraczek (2013). Are We There Yet? Improving Solar PV Economics and Power Planning in Developing Countries: The Case of Kenya, Research Unit Sustainability and Global Change, University of Hamburg.

Kenya's main electricity distributor (Kenya Power) perceive rural energy supply to be less cost effective. As such, it allocates 3.4% of its generated power to rural areas. Stemming from this poor connection, only 11 percent of households in Ngaciuma-Kinyaritha are connected. The study noticed that most rural households in Ngaciuma-Kinyaritha perceive electricity to be more expensive and unaffordable owing not to the monthly electricity bill but rather the capital requirements of connecting electricity to the house. A typical 14watt solar panel in the subcatchment cost 17000Ksh in 2006. A household head who owned a solar panel explained that the cost of connecting electricity to her house as at then would have been about 25000Ksh. Table 1.1 illustrate the comparative costs of electricity in rural Kenya.

Table 1.1. Electricity Cost and Access Levels in Ngaciuma-Kinyaritha

Technology type	Population with access (percentage %)	Required Initial cost to access the Technology (in Kenya Shillings)	Average Monthly household expenditure (Ksh)	Common model of financing
Solar PV systems	22	17,000-50,000	58	Personal savings and loans
Rural grid connection	11	10,000-100,000	120	Personal savings and loans
Lead-Acid Battery systems	9	4,000-10,000	150	Personal savings
Dry cell battery	78	100-1000	50	Personal savings
Kerosene/ Paraffin	80	100-1000	150	Personal savings

Source: Nkpeebo, (2012)

3.3 Applications of Electricity in Ngaciuma-Kinyaritha

With the price of PV solar home systems decreasing over the years, recent installations tend to be relatively of higher capacity than the preceding years (Jacobson, 2006). The study perceived that the application of solar energy at the household level is also widening to include the use of 16inch Television set, medium size refrigerator and high-end cassette players (Table 1.2). However, a higher capacity panel would be more useful for other appliances like a refrigerator, irrigation pumps and for running enterprises like hair saloon, barbering shops and others. Table 1.2 is the list of electricity consumption for commonly used household appliances used in Ngaciuma-Kinyaritha, indicating the capacities of PV SHS currently in use. Whereas grid electricity is been used for all household energy needs, PV SHS was only applicable to appliances that require less than 100watts. Thus, appliances including high end refrigerators and electric irons could not be used with PV SHS (Table 1.2).

Table 1.2 Type of Electric Appliance and Their Use

Appliance	Electricity use (watts)	Use in Grid Electricity	Use in PV systems
15 watt Incandescent light bulb	15	Often	Often
14 inch black and white television	10	Often	Often
Radio/cassette player	1	Often	Often
Mobile phone	3	Often	Often
14 inch colour television	70	Often	Often
Electric Iron	1,500	Sometimes	Not available
Small size refrigerator	80	Often	Sometimes
Electric Cooker/stove	1,500	Sometimes	Not available

Source: Nkpeebo, (2012)

Given these relevant application of solar Pv systems, it may be worthwhile considering the energy potential of solar Pv systems in Kenya. Below is a map depicting the potential of solar pv energy in Kenya (figure 3.2).

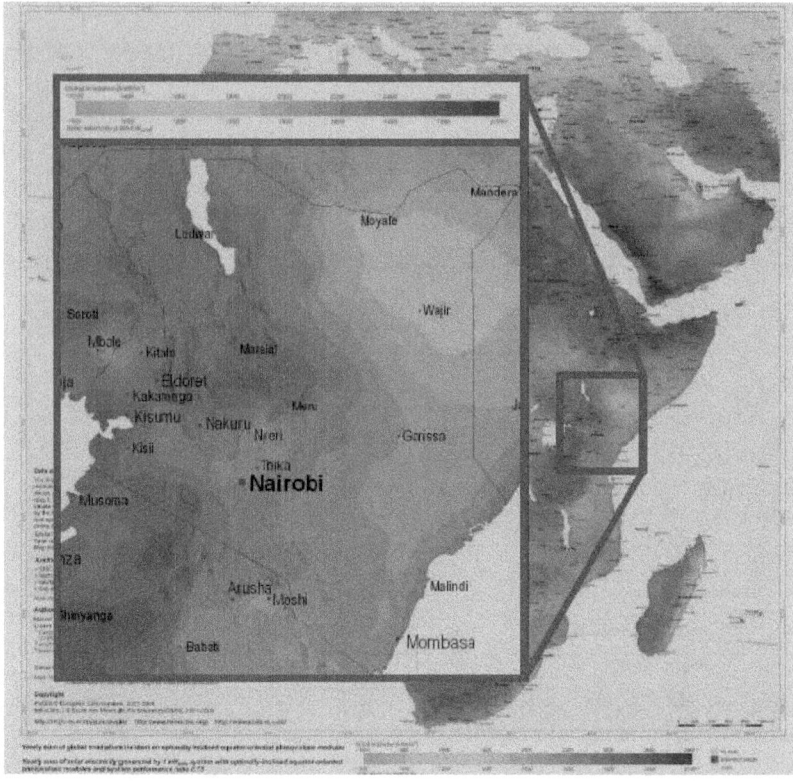

Figure: 3.2 Solar Pv energy potential in Kenya

Source: Janosch Ondraczek (2013). Are We There Yet? Improving Solar PV Economics and Power Planning in Developing Countries: The Case of Kenya, Research Unit Sustainability and Global Change, University of Hamburg.

3.4 Scalable Financing Options of Photovoltaic Solar Electricity

Women Enterprise Development Institute (WEDI) operates as a micro-finance agent that promotes savings and lending activities among women's groups in the central province of Kenya where Ngaciuma-Kiyaritha is located. In partnership with Global Village Environment Program (GVEP), WEDI is already disseminated about 400 solar lamps for household lighting. It collects a deposit of 50% of the cost of the solar lamp (2100Ksh) from the households and the other 50% is paid in three equal instalments over a one year period. This could be replicated by other micro-financing organizations Ngaciuma-Kinyaritha or scaled up by WEDI. The study also discovered that, under this scenario, 68% of households would be able to pay more than 200Ksh each month (figure 3.3). By paying 200Ksh every month, it would take an average household 21 months to acquire a 120watts SHS, costing 50,000Ksh.

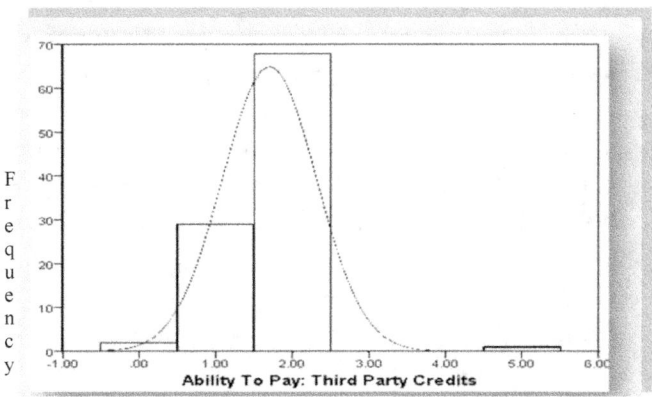

Figure 3.3. Ability to pay for SHS under third party credits model

Source: Nkpeebo, (2012)

It was also realized that with the third party credit scenario, households can improve their income and ability to pay by applying this solar energy in a business venture or enterprise and promote cottage industrialization in the sub-catchment. This would therefore require that the terms of repayment be revised periodically as the household income increases. The major challenge identifiable in this scenario is the capital availability on the part of the financiers and the lengthy legal and administrative processes required.

3.5 Observations on Solar PV energy and Rural Development

It is well understood that energy is the key which unlocks all other resources (NDPC, 2008), and that the per capita availability of energy to households directly or indirectly determines their material standard of living. Despite this fact, 1.3 billion people lack access to electricity and 2.7 billion people rely on traditional biomass for cooking and heating (Youngquist, 2000). With more than one-third of a household's budget being set aside for fuel costs in many countries in Sub-Saharan Africa, the region's population pays an onerous price for fuel (mainly biomass) that is of poor quality and not very effective for livelihood enhancement. Given adequate, planning, information availability and capacity development, reaching the goals SE4ALL initiative through the promotion of GMGs should not be unattainable. Apparently, the complex patterns of energy use cannot be dealt with by 'simplistic' linear models that current interventions pursue. It calls for multi-objective optimization and tradeoffs in energy planning and deployment which will then facilitate the development of robust business proof for GMGs. Globally, Renewable electricity sector grew by 26% between 2005 and 2010 and currently provides about 20% of the world's total power (including hydro-power). Rural areas attract a large part of investment related to renewable energy deployment, tending to be sparsely populated but with abundant sources of renewable electricity. The studies confirmed that solar PV systems deployment can provide hosting communities with some benefits, including:

a) **New job and business opportunities**: especially when a large number of actors is involved and when the solar PV systems activity is embedded in the local economy. Although solar PV systems tends to have a limited impact on local labour markets, it can create some valuable job opportunities for people in regions where there are otherwise limited employment opportunities. Solar PV systems can create direct jobs, such as in operating and maintaining equipment. However, most long-term jobs are indirect, arising along the renewable energy supply-chain (manufacturing, specialised services), and by adapting existing expertise to the needs of renewable energy.

b) **Innovations in products, practices and policies in rural areas:** In hosting solar PV systems, rural areas are the places where new technologies are tested, challenges first appear, and new policy approaches are piloted. Some form of innovation related to renewable energy has been observed in all the case studies. The presence of a large number of actors in the solar PV systems industry enriches the "learning fabric" of the region. Small and medium-sized enterprises are active in finding business niches as well as clients and valuable suppliers. Even when the basic technology is imported from outside the region, local actors often adapt it to local needs and potentials.

c) **Capacity building and community empowerment:** As actors become more specialised and accumulate skills in the new industry, their capacity to learn and innovate is enhanced. Several rural regions have developed specific institutions, organisms, and authorities to deal with solar PV systems deployment in reaction to large investment and top-down national policies. This dynamic has been observed both in regions where local communities fully support solar PV systems and in regions where the population is against potentially harmful developments.

d) **Affordable energy:** solar PV systems provides remote rural regions with the opportunity to produce their own energy (electricity and heat in particular), rather than importing conventional energy from outside. Being able to generate reliable and cheap energy can trigger economic development.

e) **New revenue sources:** solar PV systems increases the tax base for improving service provision in rural communities. It can also generating extra income for land owners and land-based activities. For example, farmers and forest owners who integrating renewable energy production into their activities have diversified, increased, and stabilised their income sources.

Ultimately, this energy interventions need to focus on how to optimize productive use of clean modern energy through locally-adaptable energy finance models planned, developed and demonstrated based on household willingness and ability to pay and marginal productivity gains from the use of GMGs in rural enterprises and to facilitate the sharing of knowledge, lessons and experiences across Western and Eastern Africa.

4.0 Synthesis of Insights and Recommendations for Energy Planning

4. 1 Energy Planning with LEAP

The Kenyan energy mix is quite vast. Yet the rural population which constitutes the majority (over 70%) is highly deprived of energy for development loosely premised on a presumed unavailability of effective energy demand in rural areas. The greenness of this argument is quite apparent in its short-termism agenda. The disposable income of rural households is developing fast due to increasing access to economic opportunities in Africa and Kenya. As a result, small households are able to acquire and install solar panels for their domestic lighting. This study posits the availability of a reasonably mature energy market potential for rural households in Kenya. The intractability of this market however, still lies in the paucity of empirical data on the rural household energy economy.

Energy planning in Kenya therefore needs to take into consideration a further disaggregation of the household energy economy in order to develop and deploy effective energy development policies. Given the anecdotal nature of the energy market potential, this study recommends the use of LEAP system (Long-range Energy Alternatives Planning model) in this endeavour. LEAP is a widely-used modelling tool for energy policy analysis and climate change mitigation assessment. This The LEAP system would help to monitor rural energy supply potentials in Ngaciuma-Kinyaritha and harmonise them with national energy development in order to reduce the continuous reliance on woodfuells and Paraffin.

4.2 Integrated Capacity Building with Multi-Criteria Decision Making (MCDM) Methods

The study recommends that, it would be expedient to approach community capacity building from a more integrative methodology rather than a perennial differentiated approach. For instance, the WRUAs should not focus only on water issues but endeavour to build their capacities in accessing renewable energy for household needs. Rural households have been observed to have a relatively low propensity to change their energy use pattern due to the limited options available to them. As indicated in this study, different categories of energy users have different abilities to pay for energy used and this differentiates their energy access levels. To the extent that individual efforts have been commendable, local development organisations like WEDI, SACCOs and other NGOs should make an effort towards harmonising group and individual efforts and enhancing their opportunities to access solar energy. A more systematic way of harmonizing local efforts is with the use of multi-criteria decision making (MCDM) methods

Multi-Criteria Decision Making is a well known branch of decision making. It is a branch of a general class of operations research models which deal with decision problems under the presence of a number of decision criteria. This major class of models is very often called MCDM. This class is further divided into multiobjective decision making (MODM) and multi-attribute decision making (MADM). There are several methods in each of the above categories. Priority based, outranking, distance based and mixed methods are also applied to various problems. Each method has its own characteristics and the methods can also be classified as deterministic, stochastic and fuzzy methods. There may be combinations of the above methods. Depending upon the number of decision makers, the methods can be classified as single or group decision making methods. Decision making under uncertainty and decision support systems are also prominent decision making techniques. These methodologies share common characteristics of conflict among criteria, incomparable units, and difficulties in selection of alternatives. In multiple objective decision making, the alternatives are not predetermined but instead a set of objective functions is optimized subject to a set of constraints. The most satisfactory and efficient solution is sought. In this identified efficient solution it is not possible to improve the performance of any objective without degrading the performance of at least one other objective. In multiple attribute decision making, a small number of alternatives are to be evaluated against a set of attributes which are often hard to quantify. The best alternative is usually selected by making comparisons between alternatives with respect to each attribute.

The application areas of MCDM in energy planning presented in this section are renewable energy planning, energy resource allocation, building energy management, transportation energy management, planning for energy projects, electric utility planning and other miscellaneous areas. Six generalized application areas and a miscellaneous area presented here have common features of minimization of cost benefit ratios, high degrees of uncertainties in formulating the problems, incommensurable units and the need to handle socio-economic aspects in planning. Renewable energy planning and energy resource allocation refers to compilation of feasible energy plan and dissemination of various renewable energy options. The key factors applicable are investment planning, energy capacity expansion planning and evaluation of alternative energies. Building energy management refers to design, selection, installation and building energy management options in a multi-criteria environment. The application normally deals with quantitative issues. Transportation system applications include evaluation of alternative strategies for pollution control, elimination of old polluting vehicles, choosing between private and public transport etc. The key features of transportation applications are of a high concern for socioeconomic reasons. Project planning refers to site selection, technology selection and decision support in renewable energy harnessing projects. The objectives are arriving at a Pareto optimal solution for technology selection, sizing, execution, investment planning. Optimal electrical dispatch scheduling, deciding power generation mix, optimum electricity supply planning are the applications of electric utility planning using MCDM. Miscellaneous applications include desalination plant selection, solid waste management.

4.3 Strengthening Decentralized Energy Planning

The current pattern of commercial energy-oriented development, particularly focused on fossil fuels and centralized electricity generation, has resulted in large proportions of rural populations and urban poor continue to depend on low quality energy sources and high fuelconsuming devices, leading to low a quality of life. Also, the current status is largely a result of adoption of centralized energy planning, which ignores energy needs of the rural areas and poor, and has also led to environmental degradation due to fossil fuel consumption and forest degradation. Decentralized energy planning (DEP) is one of the options available for meeting the rural and small scale energy needs in a reliable, affordable and environmentally sustainable way. Taking into account these features, LEAP provides the necessary dynamism necessary to facilitate an efficient DEP by estimating the end-use energy requirement and energy resource in a given region. Several studies indicate that an innovative planning of conventional and solar PV systems in rural energy projects has the potential to improve both the social and economic lives of rural communities. As such, this study recommends the following models that have successfully been used in planning rural energy deployment.

4.3.1 Linear programming model (LP)

In order to meet energy planners' need for quantitative simulation, a linear optimization model has been developed. Based on the standard method of linear programming, Groscurth et al. (1995) have developed an optimization model called 'Deeco'. 'Deeco' model has been used to analyze competition and synergy between different technologies of the rational use of energy and for utilizing renewable energies. It has also been used for optimization of solar district heating systems and for modernization of local energy systems. Basically, linear programming involves a single objective function to be maximized or minimized (subject to constraints). A Linear Programming problem includes a single objective function and a set of absolutely binding constraints. The single objective optimization approach to the energy resource allocation at a regional level has received much research attention in the past. A number of optimization models have been developed for renewable energy allocation at both macro and micro levels. Ramakumar et al. (1986) have developed a single objective linear programming model for the design of Integrated Renewable Energy Systems (IRES), where energy resource allocation for the minimization of cost was calculated on the basis of system efficiency. Others have been developed to minimize the capital and operation costs of energy supply and demand-side management and determine optimal mix of technologies for domestic cooking, lighting, and irrigation sectors in the villages.

4.3.2 Goal programming model (GP)

Quite often optimizing an energy system could involve multiple objectives, namely minimizing the cost, maximizing use of local energy sources, maximizing employment, reducing emission of pollutants, etc. Thus an approach or model to optimize multiple objectives for a given set of constraints is necessary. Goal programming (GP) is a powerful and flexible modeling tool to deal with the above types of multiple criteria decision-making problems in energy planning and management for sustainable development of rural areas. Goal programming provides a way of striving towards several such objectives simultaneously. The basic approach of goal programming is to establish a specific numeric goal for each of the objectives, formulate an objective function for each objective and then seek a solution that minimizes the weighted sum of deviation of objective functions from their respective goals. There are three possible types of goals:

1. A lower one-sided goal which sets a lower limit that we do not want to fall under (but exceeding the limit is fine).

2. An upper one-sided goal which sets an upper limit that we do not want to exceed (but falling under the limit is fine).

3. A two-sided goal which sets a specific target that we do not want to miss on either side.

GP is the most suitable technique for solving multi-objective resource allocation problems.

4.4 Piloting Alternative Financing Models for Solar Energy

Having identified and interpreted the significance of third party ownership financing model, this study recommends that it would be extremely beneficial for the MOE to begin to shift attention to solar electrification and creating partnerships to facilitate the production of bulk solar electricity in the rural parts of Kenya. The Ministry of energy is currently attempting to promote bulk solar electricity production in communities like Lamu, Lodwar, Mandera, Marsabit, Wajir and many more by giving tax incentives to prospective investors. However, much of the Ministry's efforts are currently slant towards wind energy, geothermal, small hydro dams, and nuclear energy. The difficulty is that despite this extensive energy mix, it is still challenging to reach the rural consumer and this does not only keep the energy deficit continuously high, it perpetuates the reliance on woodfuels by rural dwellers. The promotion of bulk solar electricity would spur cottage industrialization and rural development.

5.0 Conclusions

In summary, the study perceived that household energy used for cooking, heating and lighting in the Ngaciuma-Kinyaritha sub-catchment did not vary too widely among the different zones. It also noticed that, where as the dominant financing model for PV SHS is currently cash sale, third part credits and third party ownership models of financing offer a better opportunity to households to acquire higher capacity PV SHS that could be used for multiple functions including household enterprise. This means the two models have the potential to promote rural businesses and rural development in general. However, environmental consciousness at the household level was observed to be generally low which means some level of awareness creation in necessary. These two elements are critical in building a sustainable and resilient energy framework for the sub-catchment. It is well understood that energy is the key which unlocks all other resources, and that the per capita availability of energy to households directly or indirectly determines their material standard of living. Despite this fact, 1.3 billion people lack access to electricity and 2.7 billion people rely on traditional biomass for cooking and heating. With more than one-third of a household's budget being set aside for fuel costs in many countries in Sub-Saharan Africa, the region's population pays an onerous price for fuel (mainly biomass) that is of poor quality and not very effective for livelihood enhancement. Given adequate, planning, information availability and capacity development, reaching the goals SE4ALL initiative through the promotion of GMGs should not be unattainable. The complex patterns of energy use cannot be dealt with by 'simplistic' linear models that current interventions pursue. It calls for multi-objective optimization and tradeoffs in energy planning and deployment which will then facilitate the development of robust business proof for GMGs. Ultimately, energy interventions need to focus on how to optimize productive use of clean modern energy through locally-adaptable energy finance models planned, developed and demonstrated based on household willingness and ability to pay and marginal productivity gains from the use of GMGs in rural enterprises and to facilitate the sharing of knowledge, lessons and experiences across Western and Eastern Africa. The study indicates that given an enabling environment, the sub-catchment is ready to upload the full potential of solar energy to meet all their energy needs.

6.0 References

Cory K. and Coughlin J., (2009). Solar Photovoltaic Financing: Residential Sector Deployment; National Renewable Energy Laboratory 1617 Cole Boulevard, Golden, Colorado www.nrel.gov

Flyvbjerg, B. (2006). Five Misunderstandings about Case—Study Research. Qualitative Inquiry, *12* (2), 219—245.

Groscurth H.M., Bruckner T.H., Kümmel R., (1995). Modeling of energy-services supply systems, *Energy* 20 (1995) 941-958.

Gueye A., McNary J., and Okai J. (2004). Solar Energy and Rural Development: Constraints and Insights from the Developing World, http://www.gwu.edu/~oid/Solar_Energy.pdf, accessed on 8th July, 2011.

Jacobson A. and Kammen D.M. (2007) Engineering, institutions, and the public interest: Evaluating product quality in the Kenyan solar photovoltaics industry, Environmental Resources Engineering & Schatz Energy Research Center, Humboldt State University, USA and Energy and

Jacobson E. A. (2004). Connective Power: Solar Electrification and Social Change in Kenya, Energy and Resources, Graduate Division, University of California, Berkerly.

Jacobson E. A. (2006). Field Performance Evaluation of Amorphous Silicon (a-Si) Photovoltaic Systems in Kenya: Methods and Measurements in Support of a Sustainable Commercial Solar Energy Industry, Humboldt University of Berlin, University Press, Germany.

Kumekpor, T.K.B. (2002). *Research Methods And Techniques Of Social Research,* Accra, Sunlife Publications.

Mahiri I. O. (2003). Rural household responses to fuelwood scarcity in Nyando District, Kenya; Journal of International Development, Department of Geography, University of Durham, UK.

Ministry of Energy (2011).Feed-in-Tariffs Policy on Wind, Biomass, Small-Hydro,
Ministry of Energy (MOE), (2011). Scaling-Up Renewable Energy Program (SREP), SREP Investment Plan For Kenya, Nairobi, Kenya.

Owusu A. (2010). Towards A Reliable And Sustainable Source Of Electricity For Micro And Small Scale Light Industries In The Kumasi Metropolis,   College Of Architecture And Planning, KNUST, Kumasi, Ghana

Ondraczek J. (2013). Are We There Yet? Improving Solar PV Economics and Power Planning in Developing Countries: The Case Of Kenya, Research Unit Sustainability and Global Change, University of Hamburg.
Ramakumar R., Shetty P.S., Ashenayi K., (1986). A linear programming approach to the design of integrated renewable
energy systems for developing countries, *IEEE Trans Energy Conver* EC-I 4 (1986) 18–24

The Financing Imperative

Options for Developing Financing Instruments from Private Investment - Kenya

By

Amos Yesutanbul Nkpeebo

Research Group on Clean Development

ReGCDEV, Ghana

2015

Content

At a Glance

The Need for alternate Scenario in energy financing

The advent of solar technology seems to be changing this energy use pattern by displacing household dependence on paraffin, with about 20% growth rate in the number of SHS installations each year. In Ngaciuma-Kinyaritha sub-catchment, Kenya, about 6.6 percent of households have transited to the use of SHS as at 2009. Despite the relevance of these figures, it is contended that the economic and environmental benefits of SHS are relatively insignificant owing to the predominance of low capacity systems. Studies show that the initial capital requirement remains the leading obstacle to access and use of higher capacity SHS. This resonates with the argument that the current models of solar financing are not optimizing the potential of solar energy in rural communities including Ngaciuma-Kinyaritha sub-catchment. Traditional methods of financing residential PV have been insufficient to drive significant levels of installed capacity at the sub-catchment. In most cases, residential PV remains too expensive, with the high initial cost outweighing the future benefits. The operating and maintenance responsibilities can also be intimidating. However, the relatively progressive financial sector that has incorporated photovoltaic equipment into its consumer goods portfolio coupled with the removal of import and foreign exchange controls constitute the major impetus of the solar industry in Kenya. This improved understanding will serve as the building blocks for remodeling energy transition across developing countries using the Energy Transition Model (ETM) and/or the LEAP model. Finally, there is a hassle factor that must be overcome to get people to make the investment.

1.0 Introduction to Local Energy Economy and Alternatives

1.1 Background

Among the renewable and non-renewable resources, energy resource is viewed as the key that unlocks all other development potentials and livelihood advancement in both developed and developing countries (Owusu 2010). The transformation towards a sustainable economy is not only crucial for combating climate change, but also for improving the health conditions and the security of energy supply for hundreds of millions of people. At the Conference of the Parties of the United Nations Framework Convention on Climate Change (UNFCCC) in Cancún (COP16) in 2010, the international community adopted a 2°C target. Global warming beyond this threshold was considered to trigger serious environmental damage with catastrophic consequences for the planet, as well as for mankind (WBGU, 2011). A recent report of the World Bank (2012b) describes the scenario of a 4°C warmer climate with its cataclysmic changes and consequences for hundreds of millions of people. In spite of the ostensible negative environmental effect of woodfuel use and its simultaneous economic importance for about 70% of households in Kenya, there remains general paucity and inadequacy of information on alternative sources of energy or its resultant economic and environmental effect on rural household development. The increasing scarcity of wood resources and the continuous price increase in petroleum products in Kenya makes the future austere for these households and raises the need for developing alternative financing for the rural household energy economy (Mahiri, 2003). A critical objective of this study therefore was to characterize the different financing options for household energy needs in Ngaciuma – Kinyaritha sub-catchment, a rural sub-catchment in central Kenya.

2.0 Materials and Methods

2.3 Sources of data and methods of data collection

To ensure a consistent data collection and a systemised data analysis, the nested knowledge relationships approach as a guiding framework for both stages was adopted. The nested knowledge relationships approach refers to a process used for modelling knowledge units within communities required in moving towards sustainable environmental management. Primary data was collected using questionnaires, in-depth interviews and focused group discussions; composed of groups of solar energy user-households, wood and paraffin dependent households and a Local Associations in selected communities. The study also gathered second-hand data from published and unpublished materials to provide a supporting theoretical framework for guided study. Based on the reviewed financing models in this study, three alternative scenarios were generated and field tested in the sub-catchment. These scenarios include third party credits, joint community procurement and third party ownership or solar developer models.

3.0 Results and Discussions

3.1 The Green Finance Challenge

A green transformation has multiple dimensions, the most important of which is to reduce carbon emissions and to secure sustainable energy for all. This includes offering secure universal access to modern energy supplies, doubling the share of renewable energy in the global energy mix, increasing energy efficiency, and phasing out inefficient fossil fuel subsidies. A special focus has to be on developing countries and emerging economies due to the projected growth of these country groups and the related increase in emissions, combined with the strong path dependencies of the infrastructure investment decisions that are to be taken, it is crucial to select the green pathway right now and avoid lock-in effects (UN, 2013). The World Resources Institute indicates that, in order to reach the 2°C goal, developing countries will need USD 531 billion yearly up to 2050 for additional investments in energy supply and demand technologies. The Public investor challenge and Consumer finance Challenge.

3.2 Standalone finance challenge with photovoltaic solar home systems in Kenya

While there is little doubt about the size and growth rate of the Kenyan solar energy market, there is still an ongoing debate about how to interpret the significance of the current financing models for SHS, with emphasis on economic and environmental relevance. Kenya's population as at 2011 was estimated to be 41 million inhabitants with projected growth rate of 2.7% per annum. This growth is accompanied by increased household demand for energy leading to an energy deficit of about 3,000 megawatts notwithstanding its current production of 1,100 megawatts. Owing to this deficit, the current policy document of Kenya, the Vision 2030, highlights a search for alternative means of providing sustainable energy to meet both its rural and urban development aspirations. Despite the high rate of urbanization in the country, the rural sector still retains over 70% of the total population, who depend mainly on woodfuels and paraffin to meet their basic energy needs. These sources are known to reduce rate of carbon sequestration and increase Green House Gas (GHG) emission. The advent of solar technology seems to be changing this energy use pattern by displacing household dependence on paraffin, with about 20% growth rate in the number of SHS installations each year. In Ngaciuma-Kinyaritha sub-catchment, Kenya, about 6.6 percent of households have transited to the use of SHS as at 2009. Despite the relevance of these figures, it is contended that the economic and environmental benefits of SHS are relatively insignificant owing to the predominance of low capacity systems. Studies show that the initial capital requirement remains the leading obstacle to access and use of higher capacity SHS. This resonates with the argument that the current models of solar financing are not optimizing the potential of solar energy in rural communities including Ngaciuma-Kinyaritha sub-catchment. It was therefore deemed useful to evaluate the economic and environmental significance of various financing models for SHS and to analyse different scenarios in order to determine sustainability financing models that together overcome the cost challenge of solar energy use in Ngaciuma-Kinyaritha sub-catchment.

3.3 Grid connected finance challenge

It seems clear that public budgets alone will not meet the challenge. For instance, the commitment of the industrialised countries given at COP16 to provide USD 100 billion per year from 2020 onwards for mitigation and adaptation actions in developing countries is only a drop in the bucket (IFC, 2012). The aftermath of the recent global crisis, where industrialised countries all over the world are confronted with the depressing budget constraints of their home economies, the question arises whether this international commitment is deemed to be just another important target that will be cited frequently but reached only by some single outriders – just as the 0.7% ODA/GNI target that was agreed on in 1970.

Public interest has therefore recently concentrated on private investors who might have the capabilities to close the financing gap. Especially institutional investors (such as pension funds, insurance companies, or sovereign wealth funds) with their long-term investment horizon seem to be – at least theoretically – very adequate sources. The reason for this is that, first of all, institutional investors have assets of more than USD 70 trillion under management (Kaminker / Stewart, 2012) and, thus, constitute a very promising source of funding. Furthermore, institutional investors – at least some of them– have the potential to also finance long-term investments, which are of high importance for the establishment of green infrastructures (Nelson/ Pierpont, 2013).

Unfortunately, the current importance of this group of investors for infrastructure, and even more, for green projects is rather remote and even so in developing countries like Kenya. The OECD estimates that less than 1% of the assets of pension funds are invested in infrastructural projects worldwide (OECD 2013). At the same time, investments in green infrastructure projects in developing countries or emerging markets amount only to a tiny percentage of overall investments, and account only for a minimal fraction of this 1% of total investment volume. It calls to question the reasons for the degree of reluctance on the part of institutional and private investors to engage in green investments. The answer is economically straightforward: the issue of cost recovery; a challenge that many country policies are trying hard to directly address. In Ghana for instance, the government has been keen to and has already initiated actions towards reforms to attract more private sector participation in the energy sector. These include a transparent framework for the development and management of natural gas resources, movements toward a least-cost transparent process of competitive bidding for power generation, and the allocation and pricing of legacy hydro power.

Another key challenge is fossil fuel subsidies. The problem with the fossil fuel subsidies is that they preclude the creation of a fair market price for carbon, making investments in new energies and energy efficiency unnecessary and unattractive. Strand (2013) discusses and models various political economy aspects of fuel subsidies and gives explanations for the high prevalence of subsidies, particularly in autocracies and young democracies. While the former problem is easy to identify, investment risks are more complex as there are different types of risks that might form barriers for private sector engagement in green investments, some of which are of particular relevance for developing countries and emerging economies.

A third challenge that is quite often downplayed is productive use of energy (PUE). Widespread economic growth and social transformation has been an overall objective of energy finance. It is often assumed that once electricity is provided to communities, there would be PUE to boost local economic activity. However, the level of economic transformation that is expected to have resulted from electrification of districts and communities is not usually realized at the projected levels. In the case of Ghana, about half of households in electrified communities are connected, and the use of electricity in these communities is predominantly for domestic lighting purposes, generally consuming less than 50 kWh per month.

In actual fact, Roland Berger Strategy Consultants (2012) argue that the estimation of country risks are systematically too high, which entails financial harm to developing countries and emerging economies. Also, investors themselves are affected as they miss business opportunities. However, whether the assessment of the risks is correct or exaggerated – and thus, reflecting perceived or real risks, does not really matter for the outcome, as the consequence is principally the same – private investors are often reluctant to invest in green infrastructure projects.

3.4 Policy framework for sustainable energy transition

The relatively progressive financial sector that has incorporated photovoltaic equipment into its consumer goods portfolio coupled with the removal of import and foreign exchange controls constitute the major impetus of the solar industry in Kenya (Wamukonya *et al.*, 2002; Green, 2002; Hankins, 2010). However, poor standardization pervades the solar energy industry in Kenya. According to Jacobson (2001), the solar industry suffers from erratic equipment and installation standards - "Kenyan manufacturers make more than 90 percent of the batteries used in local solar home systems, 30–50 percent of the lamps, and perhaps 10 percent of the charge regulators". Due to the liberalization of the energy market in Kenya, it is difficult to regulate the manufacturing or distribution process and thus, the quality of solar home systems is not fully assured in the Kenyan market. It is worth noting that the financing modalities have the potential to influence the quality of products on the market.

The Kenya Vision 2030, the current policy document of Kenya, indicates that energy transition is primal to the realization of the socio-economic pillars within the development framework of the Vision. It stipulates that the government is committed to continued institutional reforms in the energy sector and that "new sources of energy" will be found through exploitation of both renewable and non renewable forms of energy (Ministry of Energy, 2011). The vision recognizes the fact that energy ties together the comprehensive progress of all the remaining pillars. In line with this, the ministry of energy is taking steps to integrate renewable energy use into the energy mix. One of such visible steps is the Scaling-Up Renewable Energy Program in Low Income Countries (SREP) of which Kenya is among the six pilot countries to benefit (Ministry of Energy, 2011). Hitherto, most rural catchments including Ngaciuma Kinyaritha still depend on Paraffin and woodfuels to meet their daily energy needs (Table 3.1).

Table 3.1 Energy use in Ngaciuma Kinyaritha

Household distribution by main cooking fuel (%)	
Firewood	86
Paraffin	4.5
Electricity	0.2
LPG	0.8
Charcoal	6.8
Biomass residue	0.1
Others	1.4
Household distribution by main lightening fuel	
Firewood	2.0
Grass	1.1
Paraffin	76.8
Electricity	12.6
Solar	6.6
Dry cell torch	0.6
Candles	0.2
Household distribution by cooking appliance type	
Traditional stone fire	62.4
improved traditional stone fire	21.5
Ordinary jiko	4.0
Improved jiko	5.1
Kerosene stove	4.2

Gas cooker	0.8	
Electric cooker	0.2	
Others	1.6	

Source: Imenti North District Development Plan, 2008

To attract private sector capital in bulk solar electricity generation, the energy policy of Kenya indicates that a Feed-in-Tariff of US Cents 20.0 (17shillings) per Kilowatt-hour will be made available for a bulk solar energy producer in the first 20 years. This is intended to be used to supply the off-grid stations, include Lamu, Lodwar, Mandera, Marsabit,Wajir, Merti, Habasweni, Elwak, and Baragoi and others (Ministry of Energy, 2011). According to Gueye *et al.* (2004), the simultaneous support from the World Bank and multilateral funding organizations is seen as an essential replacement of subsidized rural electrification with unsubsidized or less subsidized market based PV systems.

UNEP (2006) observed that social and environmental issues in energy use are only beginning to take root in Kenya. Given the growing recognition, the Integrated Assessment and Planning (IAP) initiative in Kenya generated three integrated scenarios (*Business As Usual, Implementation* and *Win-Win scenarios*) as an analysis tool to assess the energy planning process in the current energy development framework. The process identified the following as the major challenges to the energy sector and as such, solar energy provision: inadequate human and financial capacity, paucity of data, weakness in the budgetary process, lack of institutionalized planning process, ineffective inter-ministerial coordination and many more. All these inadequacies are paralleled through the solar energy industry as well and therefore warrant attention of research in order to provide comprehensive insight for sustainable energy transition.

3.5 Financing models of solar energy in Kenya

Among other financing approaches for solar energy, market-based rural electrification is increasingly becoming a household approach in developing countries (Jacobson, 2006, UNEP, 2010). To this effect, Kenya may have taken the lead in east Africa in. However, solar electricity still faces some major limitations gluing large populations in the Ngaciuma Kinyaritha subcatchment to the use of non sustainable and non environmentally friendly energy sources (Karekezi and Kithyoma, 2003; Mahiri, 2003),. This study seeks to establish among others, how 'alternative' is solar energy for household.

Owing to the *Electric Power Act -1997which was recently replaced by the Electricity Act-2007,* rural grid connection programs have been deprioritized since it is regarded as not being cost-effective (Wamukonya *et al.,* 2002). The same Act which liberalized the energy sector also led to poor accessibility of LPG in most rural areas leaving rural Kenya handicapped in energy supply (Jacobson, 2006). This, though indirectly, provided the needed leverage for growth in demand for solar energy in Kenya.

Though the solar industry still suffers from erratic equipment and installation standards, the major challenge for PV dissemination in Kenya, remains the high initial cost of PV products (Jacobson, 2006). Typically, the cost components of a solar system involves a solar panel which accounts for 60% of total cost; Mounts and wiring which accounts for 15% of total cost; an inverter which accounts for 10% of total cost and installation workmanship which accounts for 15% of total cost. Installation of SHS in Kenya typically costs between US$500 and US$1200 depending upon size, components and taxes rebates. A higher capacity unit may range from 3kw to 10kw usually average between US$12000 and US$60, 000 (Cory and Coughlin, 2009; Gueye *et al.,* 2004). Guaye *et al.* (2004) argues that owing to the fact that rural PV buyers are engaged in agricultural production and do not have sufficient cash in hand, most users go after the cheapest PV equipment available in the market. Gueye *et al.* (2004) outlined the different models of financing solar energy. These include: cash sales, dealer credit, end-user credit, hire-purchase and Solar Developer. Among these models, Gueye *et al.* (2004) observes that the end user credits is the most efficient with respect to meeting the needs of the rural poor. It involves receiving credit from a "third party" credit provider, such as micro-finance organizations or NGOs. This model also permits users to maintain ownership of SHS and be responsible for maintenance and repair.

Aside from the above, Cory and Coughlin (2009) highlight some "new financial models" which included third party ownership model, community joint financing as well as monetizing environmental values. Among these three, third-party ownership models is seen as the most efficient model where a Solar developer takes advantage of government tax incentives to provide solar energy from a local production station and supply it by grid to homes and institutions. This model eliminates the up-front costs as well as operations and maintenance responsibilities but it has not been explored in the growing solar industry of Kenya. The scepticism that these models are not feasible alternatives in the Kenyan solar energy market is justifiable within the boundaries of the paucity and general inadequate information. Thus, this study seeks to provide information for evidence-based decision making with regard viability of alternative solar energy financing models to foster the drift from woodfuel and paraffin to solar energy. Table 3.2 is an illustration of the framework that this study adopts as a guide for remodelling solar energy financing in Ngaciuma Kinyaritha sub-catcment based on income classes and household energy requirements.

Table 3.2 Framework for Remodelling Energy user-financing

Off Grid Homes and SME Solar Systems (less than 1 kW)	Low income consumers (individual)	Middle income consumers (individual)	High income consumers (individual)	Local Institutions
-run small home appliances, street lights, water pumps etc	Cash sales, dealer credits, third party credits, Sola developer	Cash sales, dealer credits, third party credits, Sola developer	Cash sales, dealer credits, third party credits, Sola developer	Cash sales, dealer credits, third party credits, Sola developer
Off Grid Homes and Ranches (1kW to 5kW)	Low income consumers (Group-based)	middle income consumers (Group-based)	High income consumers (individuals)	Local Institutions
For Institutional, Industrial and production demands	Cash sales, dealer credits, third party credits, Sola developer	Cash sales, dealer credits, third party credits, Sola developer	Cash sales, dealer credits, third party credits, Sola developer	Cash sales, dealer credits, third party credits, Sola developer

Source: Adopted and modified from Cory and Coughlin (2009)

4.0 Scalable Financing Options for Policy Consideration

4.1 Third party credits scenario

This scenario is based on the third part credits PV solar financing model. It assumes that micro-financing organizations and NGOs in Kenya would lend money to individual households in under agreeable terms purposely for the acquisition of solar home systems. One noted player in this scenario is Women Enterprise Development Institute (WEDI). WEDI operates as a micro-finance agent that promotes savings and lending activities among women's groups. In partnership with Global Village Environment Program (GVEP), WEDI is already disseminated about 400 solar lamps for household lighting based on the third party credits financing model. Agreeably, inasmuch as households are pleased with this financing option, they will only be willing to adopt it under terms of payment within their abilities to pay. In third party financing, the first instrument that is mostly considered particularly in Kenya is grants. Grants constitute provision of financing without costs for the project developer. The funding will not be paid back, and, in contrast to equity investments, no ownership is transferred. The persuasive strength of this instrument is its simplicity: it is really easy to implement and to manage as there are no ongoing administration costs, besides the monitoring of the project. On the other hand, the use of this leveraging instrument is the most risky one for donors: they have often limited control over the use of the capital and no recourse to it. Grants do not give incentives to project developers to deliver, and there is no return on the invested capital. The role of the public sector or development bank, again, is providing financing, and grants are very easily applicable to all kind of projects. Thus for the public donor it is a simple instrument. Project developers are most probably very much in favour of receiving a grant as they receive funding without any risks.

According to Lindenberg N. (2014), public donors sometimes resort to lending in order to mobilise private capital, i.e., they are providing a loan that has to be repaid (with interest). In most cases these loans are concessional or flexible and can thus be repaid with a lower than market-rate interest rate or with an extended repayment schedule. Sometimes the loan contract even allows for modifications. But non-concessional loans can also be used to leverage private capital for green investments. Indeed, all types of loans can serve the purpose of signalling confidence and the viability of a green project. Beyond that, they can lower the financing costs, and by this, increase the profitability of a project. In contrast to grants, loans can even incentivise project viability due to the repayment obligation. For the public lender, an advantage of loans is that the repayment can be used to fund further projects.

However, there are also some downsides of using loans to leverage private funds. First of all, due diligence is needed to verify the financial viability of the projects, which increases administration costs. Furthermore, it is hard to estimate the degree of concessionality that is needed to provide useful funding to the project without wasting public money through the unnecessary use of subsidies. Another critical issue is the risk of creating market distortions through the selection of projects. The mode of action of public loans is, thus, above all reducing project costs and providing long-term financing. The leverage ratio, however, is generally low. The role of the public sector is, first of all, in providing financing, but also in increasing the reputation of the project. Due to the weaknesses of this instrument, especially due to the high demands for project evaluation, the applicability of direct loans is limited to projects of larger scale. Usually public donors, find it difficult not only to select adequate projects, but also to identify generally eligible projects.

4.2 Third party ownership or solar developer scenario

Unlike third party credits scenario, in the solar developer approach as described by Cory and Coughlin (2009), households do not have raise capital to purchase PV module. They pay for the electricity supplied from a distributor. Based on the PESTELI analysis, third party ownership ranks more favourable among all the financing scenarios. Against this background, the study disproves the idea that it is not cost effective to connect rural communities to the national electricity grid. In view of the fact that about 74 percent of the population of Kenya is rural, the study perceives a tenable potential for rural electricity supply. Equity reduces the risk of other investors, especially of debt investors, as there is full recourse on equity in the case of project failure. Public donors that provide equity to a project are giving a capital contribution without receiving any guarantee of repayment in exchange. Equity providers acquire ownership of the project; thus, this form of financing constitutes a strong commitment. There are quite convincing reasons for the use of equity to provide financing to green projects. For projects, equity is, thus, fundamental to attracting further financing. However, the opposite might also be true, as public ownership might also signal more bureaucracy and higher standards. Providing equity entails significant transaction costs, and only if developed financial markets exist, will it be possible to exit from such investments through the sale of shares. The mode of action for the potential leverage effect works through the provision of longterm, often initial financing and the signalling of project viability which might crowd-in private investments. Still, the leverage effect of equity is fairly low. The role of the public sector, when using equity as an instrument, is above all providing finance and only to a lesser degree mitigating risk and increasing reputation. As the obligation of the public donor is high, and such a donor is consequently selecting only highly qualified projects, it might be difficult to find a sufficiently large number of projects to upscale the use of equity as an influencing instrument. Robustness, reliability and scalability are therefore constant priorities.

In the final analysis, the study indicated that solar energy is not found to be used in cooking or heating activity at the household level in Ngaciuma-Kinyaritha. Instead, solar is gaining momentum in the aspect of household lighting, with increasing installations coming to about 22% of households. The study indicates that in the year six, systems that are less than 50 watts begin to produce a positive NPV. SHS that are more than 100watts show a positive NPV from year eight (after 8 years). This payback period further accentuates the advantage of acquiring higher capacity models. Though the cost puzzle remains unsolved, in a PESTELI analysis of different scenarios, it was realized that certain potentials and opportunities available in Ngaciuma-Kinyaritha could be used to leverage back the energy deficits it currently faces.

4.3 Sharp changes in rural energy demand

Solar Home Systems (SHS) are gradually increasing in the middle and the lower zones. Energy access is also differentiated based on income levels. However, while income levels determine more of the amount of energy consumed, the form of energy used is mostly determined by availability, both for lighting and for cooking. The study noted that the form of energy used for cooking has not in Ngaciuma-Kinyaritha has not transformed much since the 2009 population census study. However, energy use has transited due to the gradual shift away from the traditional stone fire to the improved traditional stone fire and from the ordinary Jiko to the improved Jiko. It was observed that purely dependent on costs of access, about 64% of the communities prefer to use fuelwood, 30% prefer to use charcoal and the remaining 6% prefer other sources (Electricity, paraffin, Solar Panels,) for cooking and heating. For household lighting, purely depending on cost of access, about 20% prefer solar energy, 60% prefer the use of paraffin, and 20% prefer national grid electricity.

> *"If we get the solar energy that can be used for all our household needs, we can even extend it to our family members and for a small business like salon, Kinyonzi or even cold store and"*
> **(Respondent Household Head- Munithi community)**

5.0 Conclusions Remarks

There is a need for Pv solar financing to move beyond the traditional financing models to new models that may offer attractive alternatives for the households, such as the third-party solar lease model. The primary premise of this remark is that traditional methods of financing residential PV have been insufficient to drive material levels of installed capacity at the residential level. In most cases, residential PV remains too expensive, with the high initial cost outweighing the future benefits. In the final analysis, the study indicated that currently PV solar energy is gaining momentum in the aspect of household lighting, with increasing installations coming to about 22% of households. The study indicates that in the year six, systems that are less than 50 watts begin to produce a positive NPV. SHS that are more than 100watts show a positive NPV from year eight (after 8 years). This payback period further accentuates the advantage of acquiring higher capacity models. Though the cost puzzle remains unsolved, in a PESTELI analysis of different scenarios, it was realized that certain potentials and opportunities available in Ngaciuma-Kinyaritha could be used to leverage back the energy deficits it currently faces. A sustainable energy transition in Kenya would therefore mean making integrated household energy economy more prominent in the energy flagship projects of the Kenya Vision 2030. The following recommendations can be made:

5.1 Technical assistance

A key recommendation to be considered is technical assistance, which can play a vital role as a supplement to the above mentioned financial mechanisms and might include market research, business planning, staff training, or the establishment of technical standards and engineering due diligence. Technical assistance can be provided both to projects and to partner financial intermediaries that implement, for example, a credit line. The real strength of technical assistance is that it can help to establish a successful trackrecord for financing or implementing green projects. If the instrument is directed to partner banks, they should be capacitated to offer additional financing in the future. The evident weaknesses of technical assistance are the high transaction costs due to the need to custom design them in each case. The mode of operation could be simple depending on the project environment: technical assistance should build capacities both for project developers and financial institutions, and by this, signal viability for the specific type of investments. Just as for most of the customized mechanisms, the leverage ratio of technical assistance can be high. The role of the public donor clearly consists of providing knowledge, and the potential applicability of technical assistance does not have limits. In the final analysis, technical assistance is useful for projects and banks, and very often, it is an important supplement to the provision of further financial instruments.

5.2 Energy-finance remodelling

There is a hassle factor that must be overcome to get people to make the investment.
As an observation in this study, energy finance remodelling would provide insight into the unique energy packages that best suits each category. It is vital to recommend that energy producers and distributors like Kenya Power need to re-evaluate the energy-user threshold in order to develop suitable energy mix that meets the needs of all users including rural catchments like Ngaciuma-Kinyaritha including slum dwellers, farming communities, rural enterprise demand, the growing middle class and the extremely poor. Energy-finance modelling would facilitate the effective deployment of village or district level electrical distribution systems like mini-grids. Mini-grids are becoming increasingly recognised as an essential part of a

comprehensive strategy to achieve universal energy access. This is diametric to the current financing approaches that tend focus on conventional fossil fuel dependent energy sources that have less development implications for rural communities in Sub Saharan Africa. Mini-Grids are village or district level electrical distribution networks serving the needs of communities too distant and dispersed to be economically connected to the grid in the near to medium term - but densely populated to offer economies of scale in power delivery compared with individual home systems. Green Mini- Grids (GMGs) are mini-grids powered by either fully renewable or mixed renewable and fossil fuel generation. Advances in mini-grid technology and significant reduction in the cost of renewable energy - in particular solar PV - combine to make mini-grids an attractive option for isolated sites.

6.0 References

1. Cory K. and Coughlin J., (2009). Solar Photovoltaic Financing: Residential Sector Deployment; National Renewable Energy Laboratory 1617 Cole Boulevard, Golden, Colorado www.nrel.gov

2. Gueye A., McNary J., and Okai J. (2004). Solar Energy and Rural Development: Constraints and Insights from the Developing World, http://www.gwu.edu/~oid/Solar_Energy.pdf, accessed on 8th July, 2011.

3. Imenti North District development plan, (2008). District Development Plan, Meru, Kenya.

4. Jacobson E. A. (2006). Field Performance Evaluation of Amorphous Silicon (a-Si) Photovoltaic Systems in Kenya: Methods and Measurements in Support of a Sustainable Commercial Solar Energy Industry, Humboldt University of Berlin, University Press, Germany.

5. Lindenberg N. (2014). Public instruments to leverage private capital for green investments in developing countries. German Development Institute / Deutsches Institut für Entwicklungspolitik (DIE), Bonn, Germany.

6. Mahiri I. O. (2003). Rural household responses to fuelwood scarcity in Nyando District, Kenya; Journal of International Development, Department of Geography, University of Durham, UK.

7. Ministry of Energy (MOE), (2011). Scaling-Up Renewable Energy Program (SREP), SREP Investment Plan For Kenya, Nairobi, Kenya.

8. *Nelson, D. / B. Pierpont* (2013): The challenge of institutional investment in renewable energy, San

9. Francisco, Calif.: CPI (Climate Policy Initiative)

10. *OECD (Organisation for Economic Co-operation and Development)* (2013a): The role of banks, equity markets and institutional investors in long-term financing for growth and development : report for G20 leaders, Paris
    – (2013b): Using public policy to induce private finance for renewable energy projects : evidence from micro-data, Paris

11. Owusu A. (2010). Towards A Reliable And Sustainable Source Of Electricity For Micro And Small Scale Light Industries In The Kumasi Metropolis,   College Of Architecture And Planning, KNUST, Kumasi, Ghana

12. Pigou, (1938). *The Economics Of Welfare* (fourth edition), London: Weidenfeld and Nicolson

13. Reddy S. (2008). Green Consumerism - Approaches And Country Experiences, Icfai University Press, Andhra Pradesh, India).

14. *Strand, J.* (2013): Political economy aspects of fuel subsidies : a conceptual framework, Washington, DC: World Bank Group (Policy Research Working Paper 6392)

15. UNEP (2010). Global Trends in Sustainable Energy Investment 2010; *"Analysis of Trends and Issues in the Financing of Renewable Energy and Energy Efficiency" http://www.rona.unep.org/documents/news/GlobalTrendsInSustainableEnergyInvestment2010_en_full.pdf, Accessed on 8/7/2011*

16. *WBGU (German Advisory Council on Global Change)* (2011): World in transition : a social contract for sustainability, Berlin

17. *World Bank* (2012a): Green infrastructure finance : framework report, Washington, DC
    – (2012b): Turn down the heat : why a 4°C warmer world must be avoided, Washington, DC

The Behavioural Imperative

Household Energy Transformation: The link between green energy use and measures of environmental awareness

By

Amos Yesutanbul Nkpeebo

Research Group on Clean Development

ReGCDEV, Ghana

Content

The Green Energy is titled as 'Clean energy' due to its minimal environmental impact compared to fossil fuel. Solar energy is deemed the single energy resource that is continuously decreasing in price, increasing in utility and could effectively contribute to sustainable development given an enabling environment. Realising the inadequacy, unreliability and non-sustainable nature of the hydro-electricity and the theatrical cost of connection to national grid, rural households in Kenya have resorted to PV solar electricity. This could potentially displace rural predisposition to woodfuels and paraffin and cumulatively, reduce environmental vulnerability. Photovoltaic SHS are nonetheless challenged mainly by the initial capital cost disbursement, globally and in Ngaciuma-Kinyaritha sub-catchment, Kenya. The best solution to enable green investments lies in between incentive and environmental behaviour which are both linked directly to the pricing of carbon emissions. Only if we have clear long-term prices for carbon emissions, will the external damages caused by the use of fossil fuel energies be included in the pricing and investment decisions of private actors. In such an economic environment, green technologies and investments on the one hand and traditional fossil fuel investments on the other would compete on an equal basis. The relative costs of green investments would improve and they would become automatically attractive options. Additionally, other market distortions in emerging and developing countries, the causes for the higher risks mentioned before, would have to be removed to make these countries more attractive for investors.

1.0 Measures of environmental awareness and productive modern energy use

1.1 Background

Green Electricity also known as green energy, requires greater marketing attention. Although consumers are apprehensive about environmental challenges, a consistent support is rarely observed in many green products (Bahadori, 2013). The rising concerns regarding the issues of global warming, climate change and greenhouse gas emissions have raised special attention as to the development of green energy in many developed countries. Nevertheless, substantial barriers persist in government frameworks and marketing programs regarding the deployment of green electricity especially with PV solar electricity. In spite of the ostensible negative environmental effect of woodfuel use there remains general paucity and inadequacy of information on alternative. In Ngaciuma-Kinyaritha sub-catchment alone, about 80% of households depend on wood resources and paraffin to meet their basic energy needs (Imenti North District Development Plan, 2008). However, the increasing scarcity of wood resources and the continuous price increase in petroleum products in Kenya makes the future austere for these households and questions the roadmap towards achieving sustainable development among rural households. Thus, this paper seeks to evaluate the environmental significance of different solar energy financing models and to analyse different scenarios in order to provide sustainable financing models for energy transition in Ngaciuma-Kinyaritha sub-catchment, Kenya.

2.0 Research Design and Methods Adopted

The research engagements a three-part approach:

Literature review systematically synthesized from second-hand data; published and unpublished materials to provide a supporting theoretical framework for guided study. The secondary sources included journals, scientific reports, dissertations, websites, and other relevant sources of material information relevant to solar energy financing.

The 100 samples households were distributed proportionately among 9 randomly selected communities for the upper, middle and lower zones of Ngaciuma Kinyaritha sub-catchment to elicit first-hand data on behavioural aspects of energy transformation. This ensured that every sample element has equal opportunities of being selected. In each of the three zones, 10 households were selected for an FGD to provide insight for analysing scenarios generated.

Lastly, expert elicitation involved interviews with experts from universities, research institutions and international organisations. This process sought to capture more insights into the theoretical validity and practical relevance of these focal elements in Ghana and other lower income country contexts.

3.0 The Relationship between Solar Energy and Environmental Conservation

Different studies (Karekezi & Kithyoma, 2003, AEI 2010) have indicated that emission from biomass energy sources, including indoor air pollution from unvented biofuel cooking stoves, is one major contributor to respiratory illnesses in highland areas of sub-Saharan Africa. Also, as populations grow and oil prices increase more and more people in the developing world will continue to cut down trees for firewood and charcoal reducing total forest resources as well as the value of ecosystems (Schulte-Bisping H. *et al.,* 1999; Sohngen, 2008).

In developing countries where majority of the population is employed in the agricultural sector, deforestation means more than the loss of forest resources. Deforestation means less arable land, low soil productivity influenced by soil erosion and increased predisposition to the vulnerabilities of food insecurity (Fischer *et al.,* 2007). Vegetation cover has been shown to be a major determining factor in the control of erosion by influencing the soil hydrology through interception, increased infiltration, and evapotranspiration (Table 2.3). Obando (2005) establishes that erosion rate (E) is a function of overland flow, surface gradient or slope, and vegetation cover by using the mathematical model illustrated below.

Model for Estimating Soil Erosion

$E = Kq^m \ S^n \ e^{-bVc}$, where;

K (dimensionless) is a soil parameter, which describes the erodibility of the soil.

q is the discharge (m³/s)

S is $\tan\beta$ where β is the slope in degrees

Vc is the percent vegetation cover

E is the erosion (mm/m)

b m and n are dimensionless parameters, b relates to the reduction in erosion due to vegetation cover.

Source: Obando (2005); Modeling Soil Erosion and Vegetation Change

However, measured against individual economic benefits, farmers as well as wood fuel producer and consumer find no incentive for biodiversity preservation and emissions lowering. It is in line with this that Reddy (2008) and Tantawi *et al.* (2009) argue that a mere ethical standing would not be sufficient incentive an energy transition. Again, this is a question of environmental consciousness; the knowledge, awareness and willingness to make environmentally-proactive choices in energy use. With regard to evaluating the forms of energy used in the sub-catchment, the study brings to light the environmental consciousness dimension of energy use and the household propensity to transit to using solar energy.

4.0 A Review of Link between Values and Environmental Behavior

Values may provide a basis for the formation of attitudes and act as guidelines for behavior. That is, people consider implications of behavioral choices for the things they value. It is frequently proposed that environmental attitudes and environmental behavior are related to people's values (see Dunlap, Grieneeks, & Rokeach, 1983; Karp, 1996; Schultz & Zelezny, 1999; Stern, 2000). Values are typically conceptualized as important life goals or standards that serve as guiding principles in life (e.g., Rokeach, 1973). In relation to environmental problems, which often arise from a conflict between individual and collective interests, values may play an important role

(Axelrod, 1994; Karp, 1996). Pro-environmental behavior may well arise from values that transcend self-interest.

Studies show that values contribute to the explanation of various environmental attitudes and behaviors. The value scales of Rokeach (1973) and Schwartz (1994) have been successfully used for explaining general environmental concern as well as more specific environmental attitudes and beliefs (Stern & Dietz, 1994; Stern, Dietz, & Guagnano, 1995). Karp (1996) demonstrated that Schwarz's values were significantly correlated to various self-reported behaviors, such as recycling behavior, consumer behavior, and political behaviors to protect the environment. Other studies showed that values are related to recycling behavior and to people's willingness to take action to protect the environment (Stern & Dietz, 1994). In a recent study, Stern *et al.,* (1999) demonstrated that values significantly contributed to the explanation of activist as well as various nonactivist environmental behaviors, such as consumer behavior, policy acceptance, and environmental citizenship.

An area where global environmental problems are clearly linked to individual behavior is household energy consumption (Brandon & Lewis, 1999; Noorman & Schoot Uiterkamp, 1998). One would expect that in this area, where individual and collective interests are so evidently in conflict, values could play an important role. However, to our knowledge, the relationships between values and household energy use have not yet been examined. The aim of this article is to explore the value basis of environmental behavior in the field of household energy use. More specifically, it examines whether values, general environmental concern, and specific environmental beliefs are related to household energy use, the acceptability of specific energy-saving measures, and support for environmental policies. This article is organized as follows. First, we outline the hierarchical model for environmental behavior of Stern et al. (1995), which is used as a general framework for the present study. This model links values to environmental behavior via a number of mediating variables. Second, the concept of quality of life (QOL) is discussed, which is used as a measure of basic human values. Third, we argue that various types of environmental behavior should be distinguished, for these might be related to different factors. Finally, results of a study on factors influencing household energy use will be presented.

5.0 Results and Discussions

From the Upper to the lower zone, it was noticed that the source of energy used is mainly dependent on availability. The most available source of energy in a given community is the most used. In Ngaciuma-Kinyaritha sub-catchment, household energy mix include, fuelwood, charcoal, paraffin, PV solar home systems, grid electricity, touch lights, chargeable battery and other biomass residue. Solar Home Systems (SHS) are gradually increasing in the middle and the lower zones. The Naari zone (upper zone) was noticed to have less PV system preference due to low temperatures. Figures 3.1 and 3.2 are examples of energy forms used in Ngaciuma Kinyaritha sub-catchment.

5.1 Estimating Environmental Consciousness of Energy Choice

Environmental consciousness of energy use encapsulates the environmental knowledge, awareness, alertness and willingness to undertake environmentally proactive behaviours. These parameters were fed into a graded scale or likert scale to obtain interval level estimates of environmental consciousness in the study area (Table 3.1). The five level intervals used are color coded from zero environmental consciousness to high environmental consciousness. In this scale, a household was considered as environmentally aware if that household notices the environmental effects of woodfuel use or the benefits of using alternative forms of energy such as PV SHS. If a household is well informed about the effects of woodfuel use and measures that could be taken to reduce it, such a household is described as having the knowledge of environmental consciousness. Households that had taken any action, such as reduce the amount of energy consumed or purchased a more energy efficient cooking appliance, to preserve the environment were considered to be environmentally alert while households that are willing to take change or take certain actions in the form of energy transition or transformation to protect the environment were considered environmentally proactive.

Table 3.1 Likert Scale of Environmental Consciousness of Energy Use

Interval scale Elements/Variables	Not/zero	Less	Not sure	Strongly	Very Strongly	Total Score	Rank
Awareness level (1)	0 0%	2 (7%)	2 (7%)	18 (60%)	8 (26%)	30	Third
Knowledge in environmental effect of energy use (2)	0 0%	4 (11%)	16 (44%)	12 (34%)	4 (11%)	36	Second
Environmental Alertness in energy choice (3)	4 (44%)	3 (33%)	4 (22%)	0 0	0 0	9	Fourth
Willingness to be proactive (4)	4 (9%)	4 (9%)	8 (18%)	20 (45%)	8 (18%)	44	First

Source: Nkpeebo, (2012)

The study indicates a strong awareness (60%) of the environmental effects of overreliance on woodfuels. It also shows a relatively low environmental knowledge of woodfuel use. As shown in the likert scale above, the willingness to undertake proactive environmental actions is relatively high in Ngaciuma-Kinyaritha sub-catchment yet less than 1% of the population actually exercises any environmental alertness in their choice of energy. The study also perceived that about 11% were well informed about the full effects of woodfuel use including CO_2 emission, loss of vegetation, poor agricultural productivity and exposure to heart related diseases. Also about 44% have a moderate knowledge regarding the full environmental effect of energy use. This is supported in a chi square analysis at a 95 percent confidence interval ($X2= 49$, $df = 63$ $P= 0.91$), thus failing to rejecting the null hypothesis that an increased access to solar energy does not have a significant effect on the environment. The increasing use of solar energy is an indication that households appreciate solar energy Technology, apart from its environmental potential. However, the study observed a high level of consciousness with about 45 percent of respondents were willing to move from woodfuel use to solar energy given adequate capacity and conducive financing mechanisms.

5.2 Potential Environmental Effect of Woodfuel Use

Kenya's energy mix can largely be considered as "clean"; with less environmental effect - petroleum, H.E.P, geothermal, wind, PV solar energy and woodfuels (MOE, 2010). However, this energy mix is highly differentiated among different clusters within the population, for instance, the rural and the urban populations (GENI, 2008). In the case of Ngaciuma-Kinyaritha, especially in the upper foodcrop growing zone, energy mix is highly dependent on woodfuels and paraffin.

The study noted in an FGD that the level of preference for solar energy was less than the middle and lower zones and this was attributed to the low temperature in the upper Naari zone, Maximum; 22^0 and minimum; 11^0 . The reliance on woodfuels and paraffin has a multiple environmental effect. First, the abstraction of wood and forest resources reduces the vegetative cover and exposes the land to high erosion and higher evaporation (Obando, 2005). This reduces the soil water availability for plant growth. The loss of vegetation cover also means less carbon sinks increasing GHG effect. Agriculture dependent communities like Ngaciuma-Kinyaritha are the most prone to the above mentioned environmental vulnerabilities.

In the study area, though most people (55%) did not have adequate knowledge regarding the range of effects of energy use, they had the general awareness regarding the effect that energy use has on the environment. Using FGDs, it was noted that about 90% agreed to observable environmental effects of charcoal burning in the catchment. This understanding is of relevance to the environmental consciousness of energy use which is primal to sustainable energy use. In the final analysis, the consciousness of individuals or households is thought to be the most important and elementary. Thus, once this consciousness is raised, it creates a platform for sustainable choices of energy use in a given watershed.

6.0 Expert Insights on Energy Efficiency and Conservation

There is an exploration of the relationships between household energy use and householders' intention to reduce energy use on the one hand, and psychological and socio- demographic variables on the other. More specifically, the literature examines whether household energy use and intentions to reduce are important. Such examination is informed by the theory of planned behaviour and includes variables from the value-belief-norm theory, alongside socio-demographic considerations. Household energy use is strongly related to socio-demographic variables (income, household size, and household head's age) (Stern et al. 1999). Regarding energy conservation modeling, some studies have used discrete choice models while others (e.g., Dubin and McFadden 1984) use micro-simulations for electricity demand by residences and jointly model the demand for appliance and that for energy. If, as suggested in the theory, the demand for durables and their use are joint consumer decisions, model specifications that ignore this fact are likely to lead to biased and inconsistent estimates of price and income elasticities.

Others have developed simple empirical models to investigate the main determinants of household energy conservation patterns (Sardianou 2010; 2007). Fischer (2008) demonstrates that improved feedback on electricity consumption may provide a tool for customers to better control their consumption and ultimately save energy. Such work reveals that feedback mechanisms are most successful in electricity consumption. Fischer (2008) attempts to illustrate how and why feedback works, using psychological models. Relevant features of feedback that determine its effectiveness include frequency, duration, content, breakdown, medium and manner of presentation, comparisons, and combination with other instruments. Other studies examine the reasons as to why people conserve energy (Malone et al. 2002), and propose that, in order to motivate people to conserve energy, it is crucial to understand what drives people's energy use behaviour and how it can be influenced. This line of literature supports some aspects of social-psychological models, emphasizing both altruistic and egoistic motives for behavioural change. Such findings offer insights for other situations where residents are not billed for individual energy use, including government-subsidized facilities, master-metered apartments, and university dormitories.

Although it seems obvious that energy efficiency and conservation are important in reducing greenhouse gas emissions and achieving other energy policy goals, the necessary market behaviour and policy responses have generated debates (Gillingham et al. 2009). While theory and empirical evidence suggest the existence of a potential for welfare-enhancing energy efficiency policies, many questions remain open, particularly those relating to the extent of the notable market and behavioural failures. The implementation and enforcement of energy regulations in developing countries is either poorly documented or not documented at all. Such countries also lack consistent data to guide energy regulation. Residential efficient energy and renewable energy (EERE) products play an important role in energy conservation and reduction of carbon emissions (Zhao et al. 2012). The effectiveness of financial incentives in encouraging consumers to adopt EERE products is not very well understood. Efforts to explore such incentives show, as argued earlier, that high investment cost is a major deterrent to the purchase of these products (Zhao et al. 2012).

Using descriptive statistics and simple projections, Mutua et al. (2010) show that there is huge potential for energy conservation and its benefits in Kenya. This is because energy conservation can lead to saving energy at the household level and in other sectors. It is, however, necessary to dig deeper into the drivers of energy conservation. Others have evaluated the effectiveness of interventions aiming at encouraging households to reduce energy consumption (Abrahams et al. 2005) and found that information tends to result in higher knowledge levels, but not necessarily in behavioral changes or energy savings. While other studies argue for incentives as a catalyst to behavioral change, Schultz & Zelezny, 1999; Stern, 2000, make a case for values in green energy use.

7.0 Conclusion

In summary, the study noticed that, where as the dominant financing model for PV SHS is currently cash sale, third part credits and third party ownership models of financing offer a better opportunity to households to acquire higher capacity PV SHS that could be used for multiple functions including household enterprise. This means the two models have the potential to promote rural businesses and rural development in general. Though, throughout the sub-catchment, from the upper to the lower zone, environmental consciousness at the household level was observed to be generally low.

The study indicates that given an enabling environment, the sub catchment is ready to upload the full potential of solar energy to meet all their energy needs.

The study recommends that, it would be expedient to approach community capacity building from a more integrative approach. For instance, the WRUAs should not focus only on water issues but endeavour to build their capacities in accessing renewable energy for household needs. Rural households have been observed to have a relatively low propensity to change their energy use pattern due to the limited options available to them. As indicated in this study, different categories of energy users have different abilities to pay for energy used and this differentiates their energy access levels. To the extent that individual efforts have been commendable, local development organisations like WEDI, SACCOs and other NGOs should make an effort towards harmonising individual efforts and enhancing their opportunities to access solar energy. It is further recommended that household access to higher capacity SHS needs to be improved. In this it perceives that local financing institutions like WEDI and NGOs need to create the leverage taking into account the ability to pay, which is 200Ksh per month. This may require structured collection arrangements agreed to by both parties. Access to higher capacity SHS is perceived in this study to have higher economic and environmental benefits to households and the sub-catchment in general.

The study also recommends a piloting of solar cooking in the sub-catchment. As observed, the sub-catchment has shown appreciation of solar energy technology. Again, it would be the expedient for agencies like GVEP and GEF to pilot-study the acceptance and adoptability of various solar cooking technologies. This would facilitate the willingness of households to fully transit from woodfuels to solar energy technology. The study recommends that with the recent introduction of the county governance system, the municipal planning department should design and implement integrated environmental consciousness-raising programs that would filter down the concept of environmental sustainability to the household level. This would include raising the household knowledge and awareness in environmental externalities of energy use and enhancing community alertness and willingness to undertake proactive measures that promote environmental sustainability. The study perceived that environmental consciousness could play a crucial role in the global outcry for an energy transformation. This would however require a sustainable political commitment to promote environmental sustainability at the local, provincial and national levels.

8.0 References

1. Abrahamsen, W., and L. Steg. (2011). Factors Related to Household Energy Use and Intention to Reduce it: The Role of Psychological and Socio-Demographic Variables. *Human Ecology Review* 18(1).

2. Bahadori A, Nwaoha C, Zendehboudi S & Zahedi G 2013, An overview of renewable energy potential and utilization in Australia, Renewable and sustainable Energy Reviews, vol.21, May, pp- 582-588.

3. Cory K. and Coughlin J., (2009). Solar Photovoltaic Financing: Residential Sector Deployment; National Renewable Energy Laboratory 1617 Cole Boulevard, Golden, Colorado www.nrel.gov

4. Dubin, J.A., and D.L. McFadden. (1984). Econometric Analysis of Residential Electric Appliance Holding and Consumption. *Energy* 17(1): 47-60.

5. Fischer, C. (2008). Feedback on Household Electricity Consumption: A Tool for Saving Energy? *Energy Efficiency* 1: 79-104.

6. Förch N. & Ngonzo C. (2009). Capacity Building In Integrated Watershed Management In Kenya An Independent Evaluation. A Conference Paper presented at the IDEAS Global Assembly; Johannesburg/ South Africa (18-20th of March 2009)

7. GENI (2008). *Proof It Can Exist: A Non-Subsidized Market For Photovoltaics In Rural Kenya-* Http://Www.Geni.Org/Globalenergy/Research/Ruralelectrification/Casestudies/Ken ya/Index.Shtml, accessed on 8th July, 2011.

8. Gillingham, K., R.G. Newell, and K. Palmer. (2009). *Energy Efficiency Economics and Policy* Resources for the Future Discussion Paper 09-13.

9. Green M. (2002). *Solar Cookers: A Potential Mechanism for Challenging Gender Stereotypes.* Sustainable Development: An Oxymoron? pp. 62-67, Agenda Feminist Media, Article Stable URL: http://www.jstor.org/stable/4066475

10. Gueye A., McNary J., and Okai J. (2004). Solar Energy and Rural Development: Constraints and Insights from the Developing World, http://www.gwu.edu/~oid/Solar_Energy.pdf, accessed on 8th July, 2011.

11. Imenti North District development plan, (2008). District Development Plan, Meru, Kenya.

12. Jacobson E. A. (2006). Field Performance Evaluation of Amorphous Silicon (a-Si) Photovoltaic Systems in Kenya: Methods and Measurements in Support of a Sustainable Commercial Solar Energy Industry, Humboldt University of Berlin, University Press, Germany.

13. Mahiri I. O. (2003). Rural household responses to fuelwood scarcity in Nyando District, Kenya; Journal of International Development, Department of Geography, University of Durham, UK.

14. Ministry Of Energy (MOE), (2011). Scaling-Up Renewable Energy Program (SREP), SREP Investment Plan For Kenya, Nairobi, Kenya.

15. Nkpeebo A. (2012). Assessing Photovoltaic Solar Energy Financing Models and Sustainable Energy Transition in Ngaciuma-Kinyaritha Sub-Catchment, Kenya, Geography Department, Kenyatta University, Kenya. LC Class. No.: TJ 810 / .N54, http://ir-library.ku.ac.ke/bitstream/handle/123456789/7009/Nkpeebo,%20Amos.pdf?sequence =1

16. Obando J. A. (2005). Modeling Soil Erosion and Vegetation Change. FWU, Vol. 3, Topics of Integrated Watershed Management – Proceedings, pg 117-128, Department of Geography, Kenyatta University, Nairobi, Kenya.

17. Owusu A. (2010). Towards A Reliable And Sustainable Source Of Electricity For Micro And Small Scale Light Industries In The Kumasi Metropolis,   College Of Architecture And Planning, KNUST, Kumasi, Ghana

18. Pigou, (1938). *The Economics Of Welfare* (fourth edition), London: Weidenfeld and Nicolson

19. Reddy S. (2008). Green Consumerism - Approaches And Country Experiences, Icfai University Press, Andhra Pradesh, India).

20. Axelrod, L. J. (1994). Balancing personal needs with environmental preservation: Identifying the values that guide decisions in ecological dilemmas. Journal of Social Issues, 50 (3), 85-104.

21. Brandon, G., & Lewis, A. (1999). Reducing household energy consumption: A qualitative and quantitative field study. Journal of Environmental Psychology, 19, 75-85.

22. Dunlap, R. E., & Van Liere, K. D. (1978). The new environmental paradigm: A proposed measuring instrument and preliminary results. Journal of Environmental Education, 10-19.

23. Dunlap, R. E., Grieneeks, J. K., & Rokeach, M. (1983). Human values and pro-Environmental behavior. In W.D. Conn (Ed.), Energy and material resources: Attitudes, values, and public Policy. Boulder, CO: Westview.

24. Karekezi S. and Kithyoma W. (2003). Renewable Energy in Africa: Prospects and Limits African Energy Policy Research Network (AFREPREN)

25. Karp, D. G. (1996). Values and their effect on pro-environmental behavior. Environment and Behavior, 28 (1), 111-133

26. Noorman, K. J., & Schoot Uiterkamp, A. J. M. (Eds.). (1998). Green households? Domestic consumers, environment, and sustainability. London: Earthscan.

27. Obando J. A. (2005). Modeling Soil Erosion and Vegetation Change. FWU, Vol. 3, Topics of Integrated Watershed Management – Proceedings, pg 117-128, Department of Geography, Kenyatta University, Nairobi, Kenya.

28. Pigou, (1938). *The Economics Of Welfare* (fourth edition), London: Weidenfeld and Nicolson

29. Rokeach, M. (1973). The nature of human values. New York: Free Press

30. Reddy S. (2008). Green Consumerism - Approaches And Country Experiences, Icfai University Press, Andhra Pradesh, India).

31. Schultz, P. W., & Zelezny, L. (1999). Values as predictors of environmental attitudes. Journal of Environmental Psychology, 19 (3), 255-27

32. Schwartz, S. H. (1994). Are there universal aspects in the structure and contents of human values? Journal of Social Issues, 50 (4), 19-45.

33. Schwartz, S. H., & Bilsky, W. (1990). Toward a universal content and structure of values. Extensions and cross-cultural replications. Journal of Personality and Social Psychology, 58 (5), 878-891.

34. Steg, E. M. (1999). Verspilde energie? Wat doen en laten Nederlanders voor het milieu? [Wasted energy? What the Dutch do and don't do for the environment]. The Hague: Social and Cultural Planning Office of the Netherlands (SCP).

35. Sohngen B. (2008) Biofuels and Global Climate Change. AED Economics, Ohio State University, International Agricultural Trade Research Consortium, Annual General Meeting December 7-9, 2008, Scottsdale, Arizona, USA.

36. Stern, P. C. (2000). Towards a coherent theory of environmentally significant behavior. Journal of Social Issues, 56 (3), 407-424.

37. Wamukonya N., Martinot E., Chaurey A., Lew D., and Moreira J.R. (2002). Renewable Energy markets In Developing Countries; Global Environment Facility, 1818 H St. Nw, Washington DC.

38. Zhao, T., L.W, Mark, J. Sulik, and J. Zhang. (2012). Consumer Responses towards Home Energy Financial Incentives: A Survey-based Study. *Energy Policy* 47: 291-297.

The Policy Imperative

A Review of Ghana's Energy Policy Performance Using Selected Focal Criteria and Indicators

Amos Yesutanbul Nkpeebo

Research Group on Clean Development

ReGCDEV, Ghana

Content

At a Glance

There are many reasons to assess the performance of deployment policies. One such reason is the considerable resources needed to generate and distribute power. According to the National Energy Policy (2010), the energy sector requires huge capital investment (16 Billion US Dollars) to develop infrastructure in the energy sector – petroleum, power and renewable energy-in the medium term. In assessment of policy performance, a criterion is used to refer to the rule or principle on which a judgment is made, while an indicator is a property that can be measured either as a physical unit or by some other measure of quality that can show whether the criterion is met (IRENA, 2012). According to Gand (2009), the demand for electricity has been increasing at an average annual rate of 12 per cent since the last 10 years (1999-2009). Though, forecasts of Ghana's electricity consumption have been observed with inconsistencies particularly on the growth rate as argued by different authors, the underlying element is that electricity demand will increase considerably by 2030. The situation and emerging opportunities for realizing SE4AL goals in this regard is comprehensively assessed, even though in the light of the above, the Ghana SE4ALL Country Action Plan concentrates initially on two main sources of clean modern energy - Liquefied Petroleum Gas and Improved Cookstoves. The two are considered to have limited bottlenecks that can cost-effectively be removed through concerted action over the short to medium term. Considering that the ultimate goal of electrification is economic and social development, support for productive use of electricity is generally justified as a direct measure for enhancing the development outcomes of rural electricity access. Moreover, promoting productive uses can help to improve the economic and financial sustainability of rural electrification programmes and projects. However, the level of economic transformation that was expected to have resulted from electrification of districts and communities is yet to be realized at the projected levels. Only about half of households in electrified communities are connected, and the use of electricity in these communities is predominantly for domestic lighting purposes, generally consuming less than 50 kWh per month. Overall, therefore, rural electrification has been financially non-viable, has reached the limits of its success and has become a large financial burden on electric utilities. However, the policy- makers have come to believe that electric supply from the grid is right and consequently have laid over emphasis on it in the planning process. In contrast to the developed countries, in a developing country like Ghana, owing to the large rural population and the much higher levels of poverty, the provision of grid electricity is currently not yielding desired results.

1.0 Productive Modern Energy Use

1.1 Background

The absence of a specific Millennium Development Goal (MDG) for energy services is one clear indication of how the theme of energy access had been overlooked in inter-national policy processes. Greater access to, and quality of such services are now considered crucial for meeting the MDGs, even to the extent that universal energy access has been depicted as the "missing MDG" (Modi *et al.,* 2005). The development of the "post-2015" development agenda, to date, seems to have explicitly included energy. And since 2012, UN Secretary-General Ban Ki-moon has launched the Sustainable Energy for All (SE4ALL) initiative, aimed at focusing political attention and implementation capacity on this challenge. More specifically, it aims to mobilise action in support of three interlined objectives by 2030: (a) providing universal access to modern energy services; (b) doubling the global rate of improvement in energy efficiency, and(c) doubling the share of renewable energy in the global energy mix (World Bank, (2013). In line with this initiative, Ghana has set itself the target of achieving Universal Access to Electricity by the year 2020 (NES 2010). As at 2011, the national electricity coverage had stood at 72%. The situation and emerging opportunities for realizing SE4AL goals in this regard is comprehensively assessed, even though for a good reason, the Ghana SE4ALL Country Action Plan concentrates initially on two main sources of clean modern energy - Liquefied Petroleum Gas and Improved Cookstoves (Ministry of Energy, 2011). The two are considered to have limited bottlenecks that can cost-effectively be removed through concerted action over the short to medium term.

Ghana is relatively well endowed with a variety of energy resources including biomass, hydrocarbons, hydropower, solar and wind. It also has the capacity to produce modern bio-fuels (Ministry of Energy, (2011); Energy Commission, (2014). In terms of primary energy consumption in 2011, 6,138 ktoe (54.2%) was from woodfuels, 3,767 ktoe (33.3%) from oil, 772 ktoe (6.8%) from natural gas, and 650 ktoe (5.7%) from hydro. The total energy consumption was 11,327 ktoe, which is equivalent to 0.47 ktoe per capita (Energy Commission, 2014). Ghana has an extensive transmission system which covers all the regions of the country. Transmission infrastructure has, however, deteriorated over the years, resulting in transmission bottlenecks, overloaded transformer sub stations and high system losses. The electricity distribution infrastructure is extensive providing access to about 66% of the population. However, it is old and obsolete, leading to frequent interruptions in power supply and relatively high system losses. While national access is about 66%, access in the three northern regions is about 30%. The ministry meanwhile has the vision of the energy sector is to develop an "Energy Economy" to secure a reliable supply of high quality energy services for all sectors of the Ghanaian economy and also to become a major exporter of oil and power by 2012 and 2015 respectively (Energy Commission, 2010).

Given the importance of energy for development, and the high financial costs associated with energy generation, it is essential to know how energy policies are performing in order to make decisions with regard to the alignment of strategic variables within the energy economy. This article is a performance-based assessment of the energy policy and governance framework of Ghana in the context high supply variability, increasing energy deficits as well as the associated policy responses. It starts with a reflection on the energy outlook of Ghana leading into the evolving modes of energy governance in Ghana, the emerging structural variables in the energy sector, public policy responses and the resulting indications of these focal elements.

2.0 Methodology

The research engagements a two-part approach:

1. Literature review systematically synthesized the energy outlooks of Ghana in the years 2013 and 2014 linking this synthesis with the country's energy policy goals and challenges.

2. Expert insight elicitation involved interviews with experts from universities, research institutions and international organisations. This process sought to capture greater insights into the theoretical validity and practical relevance of these focal elements in Ghana and other lower income country contexts.

3.0 Energy Outlook of Ghana

a. Outlook of the Power Sub-sector

According to the Ghana's Energy Commission (EC), the total grid electricity generated in the Ghana in 2013 was 12,874 Gigawatt-hours (GWh) about 6% more than in 2012. In 2013, Ghana's peak load4 on the transmission grid was 1,791 Megawatts (MW); 2.7% more than in 2012 and the total system peak5 on the transmission system was 1,943 MW; 3.8% more than in 2012. Unmet demand in 2013 based on our projections was between 1,700-2,480 GWh which translates into 240–330 MW thermal plant equivalent. A total of about 700-800 MW additional thermal capacity equivalent would therefore be needed to cover the shortfall and a minimum of 20% reserve margin for 2014. Annual capacity shortfall is estimated between 200-250 MW. The challenge however is securing adequate supply of gas which is a less expensive fuel to make electricity production cost relatively affordable. The projected electricity demand within the constraints of the limited available supply means that there is bound to be significant supply shortfalls any time a power plant is turned off even for scheduled maintenance (Energy Commission, 2014).

The goals of the power sub-sector are to increase installed power generation capacity quickly from about 2,000 MW today to 5,000 megawatts (MW) by 2015, and increase electricity access from the current level of 66% to universal access by 2020. The challenge is how to attract investments to build the necessary infrastructure for the generation, transmission and distribution of electricity throughout the country. This is key to ensuring the sustainable development of the sector. Apart from financing, the policy focuses on institutional and human resource capacity strengthening as well as regulatory reforms required to create a competitive electricity market. Creating the right environment for private-public partnerships in the development of new power plants is essential to the growth of the power sector. The biggest obstacle to achieving this is the issue of cost-recovery, a challenge that this policy tries to directly address (Energy Commission, 2014).

b. Outlook of the Petroleum Sub-sector

The primary goal of the petroleum sub-sector according to the national energy plan is to ensure the sustainable exploration, development and production of the country's oil and gas endowment; the judicious management of the oil and gas revenue for the overall benefit and welfare of all Ghanaians; and the indigenisation of related knowledge, expertise and technology.

The Energy Commission in 2013 reported that a total of 11.6 trillion standard cubic feet (Tscf) of gas was delivered by the West Africa Gas Pipeline (WAGP) for thermal generation. This was 25% less than gas delivered in 2012 and translates into an annual mean of about 31 million standard cubic feet per day (mmscfd) in 2013. For 2014, the total volume of natural gas expected from WAGP is likely to range between 10-20 trillion standard cubic feet which translates into average of 30-50 mmscfd (30,000-50,000 million British thermal units {MMBtu} per day). In 2013, the delivered WAGP gas price9 was $8.27 per MMBtu ($8.42 per mscf) for Foundation customers and $8.38 per MMBtu ($8.54 per mscf) for Standard customers. For 2014, the delivered WAGP gas price would be $8.40-8.55 per MMBtu ($8.56-8.71 per mscf). In 2013, the average purchase price of Brent crude was $109 per barrel, 3.5% lower than in 2012.

For LPG, the total national requirement was estimated in 2014 to be within 300,000-350,000 tonnes due to the growing demand, particularly as transport fuel. However, limited nation-wide storage capacity and the inadequate revenues generated from its sales due to cross-subsidization could constrain supply to less than 300,000 tonnes range in 2014. The breakdown of the total petroleum products required would be as follows:

Product	National supply requirement in Tonnes
Total Gasoline	1,150,000 – 1,200,000
Total Diesel	1,760,000 - 1,850,000
Kerosene/ATK	240,000 - 250,000
LPG	300,000 - 350,000
Total	**3,450,000 - 3,650,000**

Source: Energy Commission, 2014

Major obstacles to reaching this goal include how to sustainably develop the oil and gas industry and judiciously manage the revenue received from the industry. In view of these goals and challenges, the policy focuses on the regulation of the petroleum industry with respect to licensing and operation of the oil and gas companies; improving Ghana's institutional and human resource capacity; enhancing local content; and fiscal incentives that will ensure maximum benefits to the people of Ghana. The policy seeks also to ensure transparency in the use and distribution of the oil revenue (Energy Commission, 2014). The national energy policy, (2010) outlines policy actions addressing regulation of the sector, mobilisation of investments for the sector, strengthening of human capacity, research and development in broad terms. It also provides information regarding the regulations governing operations within the energy sector, as well as information pertaining to strengthening the various regulatory agencies to enhance their effectiveness. Attracting investment into the sector is highly dependent on the existing governance structure; to what extent does the existing governance structure provide an enabling environment for the required investment?

4.0 Expert Insights on Energy Governance Policy Responses in Ghana

Different modes of governance can be identified according to three dimensions. The politics dimension is about which actors are involved and the power relations that develop between them, in particular the balance between public and private actors in the policy-making process. The polity dimension is about the rules according to which those different actors interact, for instance in more or less hierarchical and institutionalised settings. The policy dimension, finally, pertains to the instruments that are used, for instance soft versus hard law, the presence or absence of sanctions, and fixed versus malleable norms.

Back in 1994, along with the introduction of the general investment code, Ghana also launched the privatization of its electricity sector. Reform begun that year was aimed at ensuring an adequate, reliable and efficient supply of electricity through increased private sector investment and competition in the wholesale power supply market. Though its objectives have been slow to manifest, the reform was timely. Ghana's electricity consumption has been growing 10-15% annually over the past two decades, and industry experts predict that demand will continue rising at 6% per year for the next decade (Awotwi, 2014). Still, the majority of the country's electricity supply today is obtained from hydropower generated by state-owned Volta River Authority (VRA) at the Akosombo and the Kpong dams on the Volta River, in addition to a combined cycle thermal plant at Aboadze. The only private participation in the sector is a thermal plant (220MW) in Takoradi, in which Abu Dhabi's TAQA has an interest, and the Sunon Asogli plant (5000MW), which is owned by Shenzhen Energy Group from China (Energy Commission, 2014).

This is likely to change in the near future due to natural gas production from the recently discovered Jubilee Field and to the launch of the West African Power Pool (WAPP) regional electricity grid, both of which are set to make the market a lot more lucrative and interesting for investors. From the VRA's point of view, oil comes with gas. Natural gas has the potential to fuel our power plants and supply them at a price that is much lower than what we spend on crude oil. That should lower our costs by 50-60%," (Awotwi, 2014). This is expected to provide price stability in terms of electricity tariffs and also accommodate the volatile in crude oil price in Ghana.

The extra electricity that this gas will help generate can be exported through high voltage transmission lines to the 15 countries that will form the WAPP. According to VRA, the lines will be phased in starting in the south with Côte d'Ivoire, then running across Ghana, Togo and Benin into Nigeria. A second phase will see lines placed across Burkina Faso and Mali and stretching into Senegal. Finally, a third line will be extended into Niger (Awotwi, 2014). The significance of the oil and gas discovery is that gas creates an opportunity for low-priced power, lower than anything that these countries currently have, to be moved out there. Gas exploitation and the WAPP are opportunities that can hopefully open up the economy and improve people's lives. The public utility is also actively seeking partners for a number of new joint ventures in renewable energy projects (both solar and wind), new hydro projects, and for a new US$100 million thermal plant to be built near the gas sources in the western region.

Energy access and reliability in Ghana has received significant attention over the last few decades. Multilateral donor agencies have dedicated increasing attention to energy access. However, associated reforms since 1994 have done little to improve how actors make and enforce collective rules to address the myriad of energy problems the country faces. Scholars in this field have set out to map the array of energy challenges, on the one hand, and the (public and private) governance arrangements and norms to address these challenges, on the other (Rhodes, 1996; Kersbergen and Waarden, 2000). Yet, there has been relatively less focus on how energy governance modes can be made responsive to the rapidly changing demands in terms of efficiency, effectiveness and in some cases replicability and institutional capability. Generally, governance has become an increasingly fashionable term. One study in the mid-1990s found that the concept had at least six different uses (Weiss, 2004) namely as the minimal state, as corporate governance, as the new public management, as "good governance", as a socio-cybernetic system, and as self-organising networks. The emergence of the focus on governance (especially as it relates to development) is linked in many ways to processes of neoliberalism and globalisation, which encompasses the global shift from the 1970s onwards to financial deregulation, trade liberalisation, and the consolidation of global production networks (Strange,1996; Scholte, 2005). Where governance once used to be equated with the activities of government, it now encompasses the input of a wider range of actors from local and international NGOs, to the private sector to local participants. In its broadest meaning, the term "governance" refers to, "all the ways in which groups of people collectively make choices" (Rosenau, 1992; Rosenau, 1995; Florini, 2002). It is the process through which an organisation or a society steers itself. At stake are the functional needs that have to be performed in any social system, such as the need to cope with external challenges, to prevent internal conflicts, to procure resources to secure the system's preservation and well-being, and to frame goals and policies designed to achieve them (Rosenau, 1995; Florini, 2002).

5.0 Structural Variables in the Power Sub-sector Reforms

Along with the introduction of the general investment code, Ghana also launched the privatization of its electricity sector with the aim of ensuring an adequate, reliable and efficient supply of electricity through increased private sector investment and competition in the wholesale power supply market (Energy Commission, 2012). Electricity is the dominant modern energy form used in the industrial and service sectors accounting for 69% of modern energy used in the two sectors of the national economy. The generation and supply of electricity provides employment for a significant number of Ghanaian professionals. It is also an important source of foreign exchange earnings in the country as Ghana exports power to neighbouring countries, including Togo, Benin, and Burkina Faso. The Ghana electricity supply industry is unbundled with separate jurisdictions and entities regarding activities of electricity generation, transmission and distribution. Electricity generation is undertaken by the state- owned Volta River Authority (VRA), which operates the Akosombo Hydro Power Station, Kpong Hydro Power Station and the Takoradi Thermal Power Plant (TAPCO) at Aboadze. VRA is also a minority joint partner with TAQA, a private sector company which owns and operates the Takoradi International Power Company (TICO) thermal power plant also located at Aboadze. Bui Power Authority (BPA), another state-owned entity, is charged with the implementation of the Bui Hydro electric Power Project. In addition, independent power producers have been licensed to build, own and operate power plants. The IPP projects are at various stages of development (National Energy Policy, 2010).

The National Interconnected Transmission System (NITS) for electricity is owned and operated by the Ghana Grid Company (GRIDCO). GRIDCO is a state-owned company. The distribution of electricity is done by the Electricity Company of Ghana (ECG), a state-owned company, and the Northern Electricity Department (NED), a subsidiary of the Volta River Authority (VRA). The Energy Commission (EC) and the Public Utilities and Regulatory Commission (PURC) regulate the electricity supply industry. The Energy Commission, in addition to being responsible for technical regulations in the power sector, also advises the Minister for Energy on matters relating to energy planning and policy. The PURC on the other hand is an independent regulatory agency responsible for the economic regulation of the power sector with the mandate to approve rates for electricity sold by electricity distribution utilities (National Energy Policy, 2010).

The Ministry of Power is responsible for formulating, monitoring and evaluating policies, programmes and projects in the energy sector. It is also the institution charged with the implementation of the National Electrification Scheme (NES) which seeks to extend the reach of electricity to all communities in the long term. Ghana has an installed capacity of 1960MW with an electricity demand of 1400MW which is growing at about 10% per annum. It is estimated that Ghana requires capacity additions of about 200MW to catch up with increasing demand in the medium to long term (Energy Commission, 2012). The existing power plants are unable to attain full generation capacity as a result of limitations in fuel supply owing to rising fuel prices and uncertainty in rainfall and water inflows into the hydroelectric power facilities. In connection with this, Ghana has adopted a Sustainable Energy for All Acceleration Framework (SEAAF) to analyze constraints and identify and initiate concrete commitments and actions towards the three objectives of "Sustainable Energy for All." The aim of the SEAAF approach is intended to address commonly observed challenges in energy policy, planning and programming, such as advancing demand-driven prioritization of energy services based on development needs; coordinating multi-sectoral responses to scale up equitable energy access; and establishing inclusive and participatory multi-stakeholder partnerships to deliver universal access to sustainable energy (Energy Commission, 2012). Following consultations with SEAAF Multi-Stakeholder Consultative Group, Ghana has prioritized the interventions it seeks to pursue to address the objectives of SE4ALL, and has decided to develop the Country Action Plan on SE4ALL in two Phases. The first phase of the Country Action Plan (covered by this report) deals with interventions to promote Productive Uses of Energy and Modern Energy for Cooking. The action plan, however is confronted with challenges that may require structural changes and policy redesign to address.

Subjecting the above governance framework to rigorous assessment is essential in the given crisis situation that Ghana currently finds itself. In line with this, indicators seeking to assess various dimensions of governance have emerged, such as the World Bank Institute's Governance Matters Indicators which consider issues such as accountability, political stability, rule of law, and control of corruption (Kaufmann et al., 2010; Grindle, 2012). Development practitioners and analysts have questioned the focus on excessively aspirational framings of good governance (often modelled on institutions and processes that have evolved in developed country contexts). They have argued for a more pragmatic emphasis on "good enough governance" that meets the core functions and needs of the poverty reducing development, and encourages improvement and innovation (Baland, 2010).

6.0 The Energy Performance Matrix as an Information Tool

There are many reasons to assess the performance of deployment policies. One such reason is the considerable resources needed to generate and distribute power. According to the National

Energy Policy (2010), the energy sector requires huge capital investment (16 Billion US Dollars) to develop infrastructure in the energy sector – petroleum, power and renewable energy–in the medium term. The commitment of such a large amount of resources, especially at a time of budgetary constraints and large fiscal deficits, should be constantly evaluated sharpen its edge and increase its sphere of influence. This is especially the case for very long-lived support policies like energy policies, which may need to be adapted and improved across their lifetimes. In addition to the financial burden, ineffective policies will also take longer to achieve their objectives — meaning slower progress in providing important societal benefits related to climate change mitigation and improved energy security, among others. Governments therefore have a strong interest in analysing policy performance most especially in terms of their efficiency and effectiveness.

6.1 Criteria and Indicators

In assessment of policy performance, a criterion is used to refer to the rule or principle on which a judgment is made, while an indicator is a property that can be measured either as a physical unit or by some other measure of quality that can show whether the criterion is met (IRENA, 2012). The relevance and specific application of different depend on the context of evaluation. For example, a simple cost-effectiveness analysis may focus on policy outputs, such as increased capacity and energy generation; whereas an impact analysis approach might consider performance in terms of a country's most highly valued policy outcomes, such as long-term competitiveness, greenhouse gas emission reductions, economic benefits and energy security. As it is the simplest and most commonly employed approach, this policy brief focuses on methods that seek to assess performance against the objective of increasing energy demand. Four criteria are commonly used to judge the success of energy policies, two of which are considered critical based on the SEAAF in Ghana, including: Effectiveness and Efficiency.

6.2 Measuring Effectiveness in Ghana's Energy Policy

Effectiveness subsumes integrated resource and resiliency planning among the generation, transmission, and distribution sectors; energy transitioning; distribution and commercial loss reduction and demand-side management. Effectiveness has been seen as "the extent to which intended objectives are met, for instance the actual increase in the output of renewable electricity generated or shares of renewable energy in total energy supplies within a specified time period." (Mitchell et al., 2011). If the main policy objective is to deploy RETs, then suitable indicators are the installed capacity and the amount of electricity generated. Taken alone, however, they convey little about the success of a policy, because there is no comparison with intent. One approach is to measure the extent to which a pre-defined national goal has been achieved in an allotted period. This is straightforward and useful for individual countries. It may be of less value for cross-country comparison, because results will be influenced according to country conditions, such as resource intensity or level of ambition.

The energy sector vision is to develop an "Energy Economy" to secure a reliable supply of high quality energy services for all sectors of the Ghanaian economy and also to become a major exporter of oil and power by 2012 and 2015 respectively. A number of thematic areas the current energy policy document that relate directly to energy access are: i) accelerated agricultural modernisation and natural resource management; ii) oil and gas development; and infrastructure, energy and human settlements development. The key areas of policy focus in the medium to long-term for the oil and gas sub-sector are: employment creation; protecting the environment; revenue management and transparency; diversification of the economy; capacity development; and increasing access to petroleum products.

An energy use survey conducted by the Energy Commission in 2010 estimate d that about 40.3 % of households in the country use firewood for cooking but the proportion of households in rural areas using firewood for cooking is much higher (62.1 %) than in urban areas (25.8%), and also much higher in the Savannah (71.5%) than in the Forest areas (57.2%) and Coastal areas (52%). Ghana has been considering how to attract investments to build the necessary infrastructure for the generation, transmission, and distribution of electricity throughout our country. This investment is key to ensuring the sustainable, efficient development of Ghana's energy sector. Our energy policy focuses on institutional and human resource capacity building as well as regulatory reforms required to create a competitive electricity market. Creating the right environment for private-public partnerships in the development of new power plants is essential to the growth of the power sector. The biggest obstacle to achieving this objective is the issue of cost recovering, a challenge that our policy tries to directly address. Government is keen to and has already initiated actions towards reforms to attract more private sector participation in the energy and power sectors. These include a transparent framework for the development and management of natural gas resources, movements toward a least-cost transparent process of competitive bidding for power generation, and the allocation and pricing of legacy hydro power.

In Ghana however, Only 28% of communities remained unelectrified as at the end of 2011 and coverage of all communities (100%) is expected to be achieved in 2020 (Energy Commission, 2014). However, in terms of translating coverage of communities into effective household demand, only 64.2% of households in electrified communities were actually connected, as at 2010 (Ghana Statistical Service, 2012). As observed by Mahiri, (2003), "the switch from woodfuel to other energy forms, is contrary to the energy ladder concept, of switching from a superior quality fuel to an inferior quality with increased scarcity, or conversely, from a low to a more technologically advanced fuel as the household income increases (Mahiri, 2003 pg 165). It is therefore a well-established fact that the complex patterns of energy use cannot be dealt with by 'simplistic' linear models (Mahiri, 2003). Increasing accessibility to energy is not necessarily an indication of energy transition or transformation. At the household level increasing productive use of energy may require and integrative and collaborative approach, taking into consideration the household economy in context.

6.4 Measuring Efficiency in Ghana's Energy Policy

Efficiency is "the ratio of outcomes to inputs, for example, renewable energy targets realised for economic resources spent, mostly measured at one point of time (static efficiency), and also called cost-effectiveness. Dynamic efficiency adds a future time dimension by including how much innovation is triggered to improve the ratio of outcomes to inputs" (Mitchell et al., 2011). As with effectiveness, efficiency can be measured relative to capacity (USD per kW) or electricity generation (USD per kWh), and should be qualified by technology type, given significantly different RET cost profiles. With regard to specific policy tools, studies show that the efficiency of fiscal incentives and public finance will vary according to different institutions and countries, though various benchmarks can be found.

Energy efficiency and renewable energy are often referred to as the "twin pillars" of sustainable energy policy. With respect to the promotion of energy efficiency, the Legislative Instrument LI 1815 Energy Efficiency Standards and Labelling (Non-Ducted Air-conditioners and Self-Ballasted Fluorescent Lamps) Regulations, was passed in 2005 to promote the use of energy efficient air conditioners and fluorescent lamps. In 2008, a follow-up Legislative Instrument - LI 1932 Energy Efficiency (Prohibition of Manufacture, Sale or Importation of Incandescent Filament Lamp, Used Refrigerator, Used Refrigerator-Freezer, Used Freezer and Used Air-conditioner) Regulations – was passed to discourage the use of incandescent lamps, used refrigeration appliances and used air conditioners. This was again followed in 2009 by the passage of the Legislative Instrument LI 1958 Energy Efficiency Standards and Labelling (Household Refrigerating Appliances) Regulations. In 2011, Ghana also passed the Renewable Energy Act, 2011 (Act 832) to support the development, utilization and efficient management of renewable energy sources. The Act seeks to increase the proportion of renewable energy including solar, wind and biomass in the national energy supply mix and to contribute to the mitigation of climate change. A follow-up is the Country Action Plan on SE4ALL, with emphasis on the promotion of energy efficiency and renewable energy. In the context of these policy reforms, studies indicate that the share of hydro generation in the total power generation has reduced over the years from 92% in 2000 to 69% in 2010. During the energy crisis in 2007 when the water level in the hydro dam fell below acceptable figures, the share of hydro generation dropped to 53%. Though the country has been importing some electricity over the years mainly from La Cote d'Ivoire, it has remained a net exporter (mainly to Togo and Benin) since 2008.

According to Gand (2009), the demand for electricity has been increasing at an average annual rate of 12 per cent since the last 10 years (1999-2009). In its contribution to the claim that electricity consumption has increased over the years, ISSER (2005: p.23) revealed that domestic electric energy consumption in 2004 was 6,004 GWh but was expected to increase to 9,300 GWh by 2010 (a percentage increase of 58.9 within 6 years). There is also the potential for significant electricity exports and supply to VALCO. However, the capability of Ghana's hydro system is about 4,800 GWh and represents about half of the projected domestic consumption for 2010. This implies that at least 50 per cent of Ghana's electricity requirement will be provided from other sources such as thermal sources by the year 2010 (ISSER, 2005).

In a similar vein, Aboh (2009: p. 20-23) reveals that Ghana's electricity demand is expected to experience 23.5 per cent growth rate between 2008 and 2030 as depicted in Table 2.1.

Table 2.1: Electricity Requirement Forecast for Ghana between 2008 and 2030

Stakeholders 1970	Years			Growth Rate (%)	
	1970	2008	2030	1970 -2008	2008-2030
Total Household Electricity Use (GWh)	212	288.6	15,094	0.8	18
Total Commercial and Industrial Electricity Use (GWh) - VALCO Excluded	570.8	3,433.1	50,145.6	4.7	12.2
Total	**782.8**	**3721.7**	**65239.6**	**4.1**	**23.5**

Source: Aboh, 2009; p. 20-23

Though, forecasts of Ghana's electricity consumption have been observed with inconsistencies particularly on the growth rate as argued by different authors, the underlying element is that electricity demand will increase considerably by 2030. The situation and emerging opportunities for realizing SE4AL goals in this regard is comprehensively assessed, even though in the light of the above, the Ghana SE4ALL Country Action Plan concentrates initially on two main sources of clean modern energy - Liquefied Petroleum Gas and Improved Cookstoves. The two are considered to have limited bottlenecks that can cost-effectively be removed through concerted action over the short to medium term. In additional they are adaptable to the needs and existing consumption/buying behaviour of rural and peri-urban households - with better end-user research and targeted investments to expand supply capacity and stimulate effective demand.

7.0 Concluding Remarks and Recommendations

The recent increase of oil and gas reserves constitute a structural variable of energy policies and governance in Ghana. Growing attention to issues of governance as they relate to energy at the national as well as local levels are to be welcomed taking into consideration the fact that there are no "easy fix" solutions to the energy challenges. But there is a need for a greater focus on the numerous inter-related aspects of energy governance as they relate improvement in productivity. At the household, level and in the rural household economy, there are a plethora of variables that are less understood. Increasing PUE often require an integrative and collaborative approach, taking into consideration the complexities of household economy. This accounts for the lack of business proof for GMGs in Ghana. As indicated in the policy context, a part of the energy challenge in Ghana is the overemphasis on accessibility which as observed does not directly lead to the application and productive use of energy. In the second part, Ghana's current energy challenge is less of access than it is of reliability and productivity gains from increased energy access. This is why there is still an on-going national debate on the economic, environmental and sometime policy significance of rural electrification and by extension GMGs.

This issue spans societal complexities unique to each country that are difficult for outsiders to comprehend. This article has made an initial effort to present some of these various dimensions, and highlight some of the gaps in the current body of knowledge. Evidently, a deeper analysis of the performance factors of energy governance provides for better understanding of the potential intervention point in order to avoid the resource curse effects. By identifying the critical factors of energy governance performance criteria and indicators, our study is thus a contribution to reform energy policies in the sense of a transition towards alternative sources and higher energy efficiency in each sector of activity.

Long and cumbersome procedures: Long and cumbersome procedures for getting a connection, bill paying facility and repair facility being too far off still affect acceptability. It has also been observed that, starting from the electrification of village to the procurement of connection for the household, the time factor can vary from a couple of months to a few years. Closely linked to this is financial availability. Rural Ghana is characterized by small human settlements and given the fact that the energy requirements of these settlements are much lower compared to the urban and industrial centres, there is high cost of transmission along with severe transmission and distribution losses. Also, while close clusters characterize the rural settlements in the plains, those in forest regions are highly dispersed. Given such sparse nature of demand, it becomes economically infeasible to provide power transmission lines to few houses with a load of a fraction of a KW. Overall, therefore, rural electrification has been financially non-viable, has reached the limits of its success and has become a large financial burden on electric utilities. However, the policy- makers have come to believe that electric supply from the grid is right and consequently have laid over emphasis on it in the planning process. In contrast to the developed countries, in a developing country like Ghana, owing to the large rural population and the much higher levels of poverty, the provision of grid electricity is economically unviable. Consequently, rural electrification programmes, have proved expensive and with the constraints on incomes that exist, customers have just not been able to pay for electricity supplies received by them.

Over-emphasis on access: The SHEP is a complementary electrification programme instituted since 1989 to support the main National Electrification Scheme (NES), with the rationale of accelerating the connection of communities to the national electricity grid. Under the SHEP, communities that are within 20 km from an existing 33 kV or 11 kV sub-transmission line can bring forward their electrification projects provided they procure all the poles required for the LV network and have a minimum of 30% of the houses within the community wired. Once these conditions are met by the community, the obligation of the government is to provide the conductors, pole-top arrangements, transformers and other installation costs needed to provide supply to the community. Considering that the ultimate goal of electrification is economic and social development, support for productive use of electricity is generally justified as a direct measure for enhancing the development outcomes of rural electricity access. Moreover, promoting productive uses can help to improve the economic and financial sustainability of rural electrification programmes and projects. However, the level of economic transformation that was expected to have resulted from electrification of districts and communities is yet to be realized at the projected levels. About half of households in electrified communities are connected, and the use of electricity in these communities is predominantly for domestic lighting purposes, generally consuming less than 50 kWh per month. Emphasis should rather be on achieve an integrated resource and resiliency planning among the generation, transmission, and distribution sectors, energy transition, distribution and commercial loss reduction, promotion of energy efficiency and demand-side management and support for the expansion of renewable energy projects. Ghana requires improving the creditworthiness of the ECG and NEDCo. Again, Mini-grids are becoming increasingly recognised as an essential part of a comprehensive strategy to achieve universal energy access and an integrated resource planning should take into account GMGs. Green Mini- Grids (GMGs) are mini-grids powered by either fully renewable or mixed renewable and fossil fuel generation. Advances in mini-grid technology and significant reduction in the cost of renewable energy - in particular solar PV - combine to make mini-grids an attractive option for isolated sites. Profitable and sustainable deployment of GMGs in Ghana is highly contingent on enhancing productive uses of energy and increasing productivity gains generated from electricity access.

8.0 References

1. Baland J-M, Moene KO, Robinson JA. (2010). Governance and development. In: Rodrik D, Rosenzweig MR, editors. Handbook of development economics, vol. 5.Oxford, UK: Elsevier.

2. Bradbrook AJ, Gardam JG., (2006). Placing access to energy services within a human rights framework. Hum Rights Q 2006;28(2):389–415.

3. Delina LL. (2012). Coherence in energy efficiency governance. Energy Sustain Dev. 16(4):493–9.

4. Energy Commission, (2014) Energy (Supply And Demand) Outlook for Ghana

5. Ernst & Young, (2014). Rapid Growth Markets Report on Ghana, February, 2014; IMF report on Ghana economy, February, 2014; NDPC, GSGDA II.

6. Florini A. The coming democracy: new rules for running a new world. Washington, DC: Island Press; 2003.

7. Florini A, Dubash NK. (2011). Introduction to the special issue: governing energy in a fragmented world. Glob Policy 2011;2(s1).

8. Grindle M. (2012). Good governance: the inflation of an idea. In: Sanyal B, Vale L J, Rosan C, editors. Planning ideas that matter: livability, territoriality, governance, and reflective practice. Cambridge, MA: MIT Press; 2012.p. 259.

9. Goldthau A. (2014). Rethinking the governance of energy infrastructure: scale, decentralization and polycentrism. Energy Res Soc Sci 2014;1:134–40.

10. IEA. (2012). World energy outlook 2013. Paris: OECD/IEA; 2013.

11. Kaufmann D, Kraay A, Mastruzzi M. The worldwide governance indicators: a summary of methodology, data and analytical issues. World Bank Policy Res Working Paper 5430; 2010.

12. Kaufmann D, Kraay A, Zoido-Lobaton P. (2010). Governance matters. World Bank Policy Research Working Paper No. 2196. Washington, DC: The World Bank.

13. Kersbergen Kv, Waarden Fv. (2004). 'Governance' as a bridge between disciplines: cross-disciplinary inspiration regarding shifts in governance and problems of governability, accountability and legitimacy. Eur J Pol Res2004;43(2):143–71.

14. Ministry of Energy, (2011). National Electrification Scheme (NES) Master Plan Review (2011-2020) Final.

15. Modi V, McDade S, Lallement D, Saghir J. (2005). Energy services for the millennium development goals. New York: Energy Sector Management Assistance Programme, United Nations Development Programme, UN Millennium Project, and World Bank; 2005.

16. National Electrification Scheme (NES), (2010). Ministry of Energy, Ghana, Accra.

17. National Development Planning Commission, NDPC (2010). Ghana Shared Growth and Development Agenda (GSGDA), 2010-2013 Volume I: Policy Framework

18. Phillips J, Newell P. (2013). The governance of clean energy in India: the clean development mechanism (CDM) and domestic energy politics. Energy Policy 2013;59: 654–62.

19. Rhodes RAW. (1996). The new governance: governing without government1. Pol Stud1996;44(4):652–67.

20. Rosenau JN, Czempiel E-O. (1992). Governance without government: order and change in world politics, vol. 20. Cambridge, UK: Cambridge University Press; 1992.

21. Rosenau JN. (1995). Governance in the twenty-first century. Glob Gov 1995;1:13.

22. Scholte JA. (2005). Globalization: a critical introduction. Palgrave: Macmillan; 2005.

23. Strange S. (1996). The retreat of the state: the diffusion of power in the world econ-omy. Cambridge, UK: Cambridge University Press.

24. Strategic National Energy Plan (2006-2020), Energy Commission, available at www.energycom.gov.gh.

25. Sovacool BK, Cooper CJ. (2013). The governance of energy megaprojects: politics, hubris and energy security. London: Edward Elgar Publishing.

26. Transparency International. (2014). Corruption perception index; 2013 [cited 2015 February 25] Available from: http://cpi.transparency.org/cpi2013/in detail/

27. Treib O, Bähr H, Falkner G. (2007). Modes of governance: towards a conceptual clarification. J EurPubl Policy 2007;14(1):1–20.

28. Verdonk M, Dieperink C, Faaij APC. (2007). Governance of the emerging bio-energy markets. Energy Policy 2007;35(7):3909–24.

29. Weiss TG. (2000). Governance, good governance and global governance: conceptual and actual challenges. Third World Q 2000;21(5):795–814.

30. World Bank, (2013). Global tacking framework – sustainable energy for all. Washington, DC: World Bank